Harry Harrison

Twayne's United States Authors Series

Warren French, Editor

University of Wales, Swansea

TUSAS 560

HARRY HARRISON
Photograph by Jerry Bauer, © *1984.*

Harry Harrison

By Leon Stover

Illinois Institute of Technology

Twayne Publishers
A Division of G. K. Hall & Co. • Boston

Harry Harrison
Leon Stover

Copyright 1990 by G. K. Hall & Co.
All rights reserved.
Published by Twayne Publishers
A Division of G. K. Hall & Co.
70 Lincoln Street
Boston, Massachusetts 02111

Book production by Janet Z. Reynolds.
Book design by Barbara Anderson.
Typeset in 11 pt. Garamond
by Compositors Corp., Cedar Rapids, Iowa.

Printed on permanent/durable acid-free paper
and bound in the United States of America.

First published, 1990.
10 9 8 7 6 5 4 3 2 1

Library of Congress Cataloging-in-Publication Data
Stover, Leon E.
     Harry Harrison / by Leon Stover.
        p.   cm. — (Twayne's United States authors series ; TUSAS 560)
     Includes bibliographical references.
     ISBN 0-8057-7603-6 (alk. paper)
     1. Harrison, Harry—Criticism and interpretation.   2. Science
fiction, American—History and criticism.   I. Title.   II. Series.
PS3558.A667Z87   1990
813'.54—dc20   89-27438
                                                                                    CIP

For
Takeko, as usual,
and for
Robert Asher,
our helpful family friend

Contents

About the Author

Leon Stover is professor of anthropology at Illinois Institute of Technology, where he began teaching courses on science fiction in 1965. In 1972 he was commissioned by the Sorbonne to write *La Science Fiction Amèricaine,* a textbook in its American studies program.

Before coming to Chicago he was for two years a visiting professor at Tokyo University, invited by its graduate school to teach sinological theory. His lectures there are published as *The Cultural Ecology of Chinese Civilization* (1974) and, with the help of Mrs. Takeko Kawai Stover, are expanded in *China: An Anthropological Perspective* (1976). Thereafter he turned to European prehistory with *Stonehenge and the Origins of Western Culture* (1979). But he first played with his new ideas about that monument in the novel *Stonehenge* (1972), done with Harry Harrison, later enlarged as *Stonehenge: Where Atlantis Died* (1983). The two of them also edited a theme anthology on the topic of anthropological science fiction, *Apeman, Spaceman* (1968).

Stover is the author of *The Prophetic Soul: A Reading of H. G. Wells's "Things to Come"* (1987), and on the fiftieth anniversary of *Things to Come* he lectured at the National Film Theatre by invitation of the British Film Institute. Earlier he did a work of Wellsian literary criticism in the form of a dialogue novel, *The Shaving of Karl Marx* (1982). The publication of his *Robert A. Heinlein* in 1987 was followed in 1988 by his appointment as Heinlein's authorized biographer.

Stover holds a Ph.D. in anthropology and China studies from Columbia University and was awarded an honorary Litt.D. from Western Maryland College, where he earned his undergraduate degree in English.

Foreword

An Appreciation of Harry Harrison

In 1987 Harry Harrison was guest of honor at Windycon XIII, a regional science fiction conference held in the Chicago area. He was introduced from afar by the British master Brian Aldiss. What follows is Aldiss's "Guest-of-Honor Appreciation," the standard locution at such gatherings that was printed in a souvenir program issued at the time. Aldiss has added some remarks he wrote especially for this book in September 1988.

When I was asked to write 750 words on your Guest of Honor, Harry Harrison, several of them sprang to mind straightaway: gallant, creative, ebullient, eudemonistic, witty, plantigrade, multifarious, tough, staunch, shy, eloquent, uproarious, homothermic—

But stop! That's enough. Let's track back to the creative bit.

Maybe you need reminding (or maybe you don't) that Harry Harrison is one of the long-standing, record-breaking giants in the SF field. He charged into print in the great days of John Campbell and has been unstoppable ever since. He began as an artist, he once wrote the storylines for good old Flash Gordon, and he has edited a thousand legendary anthologies—some of them with a sliver of help from me.

There's hardly a thing Harry hasn't done, and done well. Look at the list of his novels. Not a dud among them, and many a masterpiece. Although he's now so famous for the Stainless Steel Rat books, you youngsters attending your first convention and saving up to buy your first razor should seek out early Harrisons, which have matured like good vintage wine.

Like: the *Deathworld* trilogy, *Make Room! Make Room!*, and all the early group of funnies, *Bill, the Galactic Hero, The Technicolor Time Machine*, and *Tunnel through the Deeps*. Plus a dozen more I could name. They rank among the best SF novels ever written.

So how come Harry hasn't got a whole shelf full of Hugos and Nebulas? I grow angry at this question, and let me tell you the answer throws no rosy light on those who vote for such trophies.

The fact is, Harry is a great traveller, an exile in the best sense of the word, with a true science-fictional sense (granted to few SF writers) that every corner of the world is his home. So while young Joe Soap, the latest "favourite writer" of the clan and author of a six-volume trilogy, is touring conventions and buttering up readers to vote for Soap books, where's Harrison? Why, Harrison's away—two fathoms down, touring the Great Barrier Reef with oxygen tank and flippers, or charming all Bejing with his mastery of Mandarin and Esperanto.

So Harry and his charming and jolly wife, Joan, have been all around the globe, living here and there, often in delightful places worth a ton of Hugos.

Harry's cheery approach to life breaks down barriers and sobriety wherever he goes. I remember once when Margaret and I were traveling with Harry and Joan in the Croatian sector of Jugoslavia and we arrived at a fairly godforsaken port on the Istran peninsula. We really hoped to be somewhere else. We stopped on a cliff where people were either promenading or thinking about hurling themselves into the Adriatic.

Out jumps Harry, buttonholes one of the passing guys, and immediately starts an immense conversation bristling with gestures and sound effects, punctuated with laughter. The rest of us sit tight in the vehicle, wondering vaguely how Harry came to be a secret master of Serbo-Croat.

After about an hour, Harry comes back to the buggy, still smiling, and says, "Okay, he says there's a good cheap hotel just down the road where we can stay. Easiest way to get there is drive the wrong way down their one-way system."

"Harry," I say, plaintively, "what was that about?"

He has been talking to the man in Esperanto.

"The poor sod works down in a Croatian coalmine. He was telling me how awful it was. Brian, have you ever thought what life must be like down a Croatian coalmine?!"

Somewhere buried in the Stainless Steel Rat books you will find what is manifestly a comic description of a Croatian coalmine. Harry enjoys, as I do, the more awful broken-down aspects of life, and such touches of real experience add flavour to his narrative. You will remember, of course, that Esperanto—as The Bishop reminds Jim in *A Stainless Steel Rat Is Born*—is "the galactic language, the simple, second language that everyone learns early and speaks like a native. . . ." If it worked on the Istran peninsula, why not in Outer Space?

But the surest proof of Harry's marvelous comic genius is—

Hang on, though, I've done 750 words, and that's all Harry's paying me for. Besides, you'll discover his comic genius for yourselves during Windycon. Over to you, Harry, old chum!

*   *   *

This friendly little piece was written for an informal occasion. Within the formal occasion of this study of Harrison's writing, to write something more formal is difficult, so long have Harrison and I been acquainted. It is not for me to evaluate his writing, since my response to it is naturally an emotional one.

I have many many American friends. Of these, Harry was there first, and remains there, a quarter of a century later. Someone said that friends are the people who get to you first. This may sound cynical, but I believe it is more than that; in any case, because a thing is cynical is not to say it is untrue. It's one thing to get there first, and quite another to remain there. Just as it is easy to become a writer but another to remain one. (I frighten aspiring writers by telling them that.)

There is a soft side to writing. To anyone working down a mine or building a motorway, our job of sitting at a desk must seem remarkably soft. Okay, try it for thirty years.

What do you need for such endurance? Well, you need stamina, determination, and a lot of hope. You also need something to say.

You might think that an author's dilemma would be that he would soon run out of material. For many writers, it is like that. They have nothing more to say after five or six books, after which they have to reinvent constantly new or fairly new ways of saying the old things over. That crucifies. Half the professional writers writing today hate their typewriters or their word processors.

Harrison has not run out of valid things to say. From one book unfolds the next. Book T cannot be written before Book S, or Book U before Book T. By which algebraic example I do not mean to imply that Harrison is reaching the end of his alphabet. I hope he never does so. I do imply that his books represent a continuity, although—this is no paradox—the underlying train of thought remains constant. We all have one or two subjects to which we return, as Dostoyevski returned to the inexhaustible subject of justice, lay and holy.

And Harrison's subject? I'd say: survival. Ways of survival in a number of different environments, all of them in some way hostile to the individual. This is the Harrisonian song. It serves him well. It is a subject of immediate relevance to all of us. Hence, I suppose, his enduring popularity.

Brian Aldiss

Preface

The week after Christmas in 1972, Auberon Waugh at the *Spectator* received just one novel to review. Written by an author he had never heard of, it belonged to a genre he long had dismissed as a witless form of proletarian entertainment. Why his intelligent friend, Kingsley Amis, took an interest in science fiction was a puzzler—until that solitary book came across his desk in the slack season. Mr. Waugh read it, with astonishment. "It is very seldom indeed in a novel reviewer's experience that he has the feeling of Keats on first looking into Chapman's Homer." Finding the story "immensely satisfying," he concluded his review with the words, "It is a book which I can recommend with all my heart." His review is reprinted as the introduction to the New English Library edition (1976) of the book in question: a comic, alternate-world novel titled, *A Transatlantic Tunnel, Hurrah!* After reading *Skyfall* "in a single all-night gulp," the famous British novelist Anthony Burgess wrote to Harry Harrison praising his "scientific knowledge and power to imagine this kind of set-up" and "capacity to write clearly" so enthusiastically that the delighted author had the encomium framed and hung on his study wall.

I quote from the Waugh review and the Burgess letter to make a point that is almost shameful to have to make. While Harrison is one of the most popular living science fiction writers, measured in terms of mass readership and sales, he is a nonsubject in the literature of academic science fiction criticism. Yet a few authors of more limited appeal are favored for treatment over and over again. Indeed, to one such author the scholars of the Science Fiction Research Association have devoted no less than seven books. About Harry Harrison, not one; not even one article. Genteel critics had the same lofty disdain for Mark Twain's commercial success in his day—if popular, he cannot be any good.

This book aims to set the record right. But there is nothing to cite in my secondary sources except the eight fanzine issues of the Harry Harrison Appreciation Society and its ten newssheets, and general studies.

Further to defend my own taste and to buttress my critical judgments, I have begun by calling upon a science fiction writer of indefeasible authority, Brian Aldiss, who speaks for all Harry Harrison's admirers. Despite my prefatory deference to these masters, this book is based exclusively on my own reading or, rather, close rereading of Harrison's oeuvre, for I have been long acquainted with the man and his works, title by title as they appeared. More-over, I have collaborated with him on three books. Beyond that, I spent two weeks taking notes during daily interviews with him in the summer of 1988, since one of the matters that most interested me is the genesis of his books and story ideas. Quotations from Harrison, not otherwise identified, are from these interviews. Citations from Harrison's books are located by chapter rather than page references because of the variety of editions in which his works have appeared.

My acknowledgments, or rather those of Mrs. Stover and myself (she being my comrade in this as in all other projects), therefore must first of all place us in the debt of Harry and Joan Harrison, whose hospitality was of-fered for such a long time. We are no less grateful to their daughter, Moira, Mrs. Guillot, for putting us up over the nights in her next-door cottage, lo-cated on a working farm in Cornwall, England. Her husband we saw only once, following his return from some distant job of forestry management, but we are thankful for that brief meeting and his warm endorsement of our prolonged presence there at Prospect Farm.

To Paul Tomlinson, the young student founder from Nottingham of the Harry Harrison Appreciation Society, I am indebted for his outstanding gen-erosity in sharing with me his working manuscript on a complete bibliogra-phy (including all editions and foreign translations), to be published by the Borgo Press in California.

And to Brian Aldiss, my dearest thanks for meeting the need he knew I felt.

Happily, the merits of my proposal for this book were recognized by War-ren French, on behalf of Twayne Publishers. Indeed, he and I and Mr. Harrison were all brought together for a weekend at Prospect Farm for a meeting between editor, critic, and subject, the first that has ever been held in connection with any title in this series. Once again, as with the *Robert Heinlein* title of 1987, I am obliged to Professor French for his astute editing and wise counsel. What the nameless copy editor has done beyond that is less philosophical, yet essential, if the formal dignities of the series format are to be upheld.

Leon Stover

Illinois Institute of Technology

Chronology

1925   Henry Maxwell Dempsey (Harry Harrison) born 12 March in Stamford, Connecticut, the only child of Ria Kirjassoff and Henry Leo Dempsey.

1938   Becomes charter member of the Queens chapter of the Science Fiction League.

1943   Graduates from Forest Hills High School.

1943–1948   Serves in U.S. Army Air Corps as a technical specialist.

1946–1948   Attends Cartoonists and Illustrators School on the G.I. Bill, and studies independently under the painter John Blomshield.

1946–1955   Works as free-lance commercial artist in New York City.

1950   4 July: chairs Hydracon, in New York City, the first professional science fiction writers convention.

1951   Publishes first science fiction story, "Rock Diver."

1954   4 June: marries Joan Merkler.

1955   21 May: birth of son, Todd Harrison.

1955–1958   Lives in Mexico, England, and Italy, before returning to New York City, as a free-lance writer.

1958–1968   Scripts the story for the revived "Flash Gordon" comic strip.

1959   9 January: birth of daughter, Moira Harrison. Summer: moves to Denmark, where he lives until 1965.

1960   Publishes first novel, *Deathworld*.

1961   *The Stainless Steel Rat*, the first of a popular series (whose latest title—as of 1989—is *The Stainless Steel Rat Gets Drafted*).

1964   With Brian Aldiss, founds *SF Horizons*, the first magazine of science fiction criticism.

1965   *Bill, the Galactic Hero*, written in Denmark, is published while living in London (from 1965 to 1966).

1966   *Make Room! Make Room!*, a serious novel about overpopulation.

1967   *The Technicolor Time Machine*, a comic adventure novel.

1967–1974   Lives in suburbs of San Diego, California.

1968–1976   With Brian Aldiss, edits nine volumes of a year's best science fiction series.

1969   *Captive Universe,* his most "literary" novel, is an April Book-of-the-Month Club selection.

1973   Wins Nebula Award, presented by Science Fiction Writers of America, for the film story *Soylent Green,* based on *Make Room! Make Room!.*

1975   Begins permanent residence in Ireland.

1976   *The Best of Harry Harrison,* a collection of stories distilled from previous collections.

1976   In Dublin, organizes the First International Science Fiction Authors Conference.

1977   Elected president of the newly-founded World SF.

1985   Elected honorary patron of the Universal Esperanto Association.

1984–1988   *West of Eden* trilogy, the crowning work of Harrison's career to date.

1990   Guest of honor at the 48th World Science Fiction Convention, held in The Hague.

Chapter One
Science Fiction and the Research Revolution

Science fiction is an American publisher's category, created for the speciality magazines. The first specialty magazines, the so-called dime novels, appeared in the 1840s and established the specialized categories of fiction now tagged western, romance, crime, etc. The dime novel entered a boom period in the 1870s; the prominent publishers were the house of Beadle and Adams, and especially Frank Tousey. Number 451 of Tousey's Wide Awake Library, for example, is entitled *The True Life of Billy the Kid*, issued in 1881. It is a booklet of sixteen pages, measuring eight by twelve inches, and set in very small type. The cover is printed with crude steel-plate engraving. Price: five cents (some other dime novels cost up to twenty-five cents). The inside cover lists several hundred of the 1,353 titles published by Tousey. *The True Life of Billy the Kid*, altogether fictional, is an example of the western genre. Other genres included in The Wide Awake Library are pirate stories, sea stories, city stories about high life or low life, and stories of exploration, adventure, and romance.

Another dime novel series, Beadle's Popular Library, advertised the following genres: wild west, border, mining, ranching, secret service, detective, robber, city, and sea life. Dime novels sold in the millions, and the industry hired hundreds of hack writers who specialized in producing one category or another.

The dime novel died out by the turn of the century and was replaced by the pulp magazine. Its standard format was 120 untrimmed pages of rough woodpulp paper, measuring seven by ten inches, with an enameled cover and interior illustrations. The price ranged from ten to twenty-five cents. At its height during the 1920s and 1930s, the pulp magazine industry numbered unknown hundreds of titles and sold about twenty million copies a month.

The first of the pulps was *Argosy*, an adventure story magazine, started in 1896. Street and Smith Publications, a rival of Tousey's that the former eventually absorbed, originated three more pulp magazines: *Detective Story* (1915), *Western Story* (1919), and *Love Story* (1921). The four categories of adventure, detective, western, and romance dominated the pulps until they in turn yielded to paperback books during the 1940s. The categories they carried forward have now passed into television programming.

Invention Stories

Into the pulp market at its peak came *Amazing Stories*. The editor and publisher was Hugo Gernsback, the father of magazine science fiction. The first issue appeared in April 1926 and sold over a hundred thousand copies—a good share of the market. It soon was imitated by the magazines *Astounding, Astonishing, Startling,* and *Thrilling.* By the 1950s more than ninety magazines were in the field—quite a few more titles than there were synonyms for "amazing" in *Roget's Thesaurus.*

Science fiction readers had always known what to expect in the magazine of their choice, and their loyalties were as focused as the favored genre was specialized. Readers were in fact not just readers any longer but "fans," short for fanatics.

What new species of loyalty did Hugo Gernsback cultivate in science fiction fans? What amazing things did they expect to find in *Amazing Stories*, issue after issue? The answer is, amazing inventions. Across the magazine's masthead ran the slogan "Extravagant Fiction Today . . . Cold Fact Tomorrow." For Hugo Gernsback, science fiction—or "scientific fiction" as he called it up until 1929—was a trade name for invention stories.

Invention stories, however, did not originate with him. They go back, as do so many of the categories of pulp fiction, to the dime novel. In this case, to another one of Frank Tousey's dime novel series, The Frank Reade Library, which ran between 1892 and 1898. Frank Reade, boy inventor and backyard gadgeteer, who cobbles up things like steam-operated mannikins to do household chores and pull the family buggy, is modeled after young Tom Edison, king of inventors, modern magician, and wizard of Menlo Park. But this was before anyone had the historical perspective to see that Edison was no naively inventive gadgeteer working in the tradition of "Yankee ingenuity," much less a wizard working in the chancy alchemical tradition. His "invention factory" at Menlo Park was emphatically a factory, organized along the lines of group research for the purpose of turning out new products to meet evident commercial needs of the marketplace. His grasp of the problem of electric lighting, as a system to replace the system of gas lighting, shows that fact. The electric light bulb was no accidental flash of intuitive genius, but the product of a larger purpose; it was designed as part of a system that included a network of electric power lines and a central power station. Edison began working on all these problems at the same time, and in 1878 his invention factory was incorporated as the Edison Electric Light Company, out of which grew the General Electric Company, formed in 1892.

It was Edison's concept of group research, not the spirit of the lone inventor, to which *Amazing Stories* was a response. Or at least a belated response. Before the first science fiction magazine could capture a market of fans interested in the romance of industrial research, the idea itself had to be popularized and embodied in widespread practice.

If Edison was the first American to organize group research, its first missionary was Arthur D. Little, who took it upon himself (in his own words) "to preach the Gospel of Research." He traveled all over North America, preaching to manufacturing firms, chambers of commerce, and scientific associations. "Research," Little said, "is the mother of industry." At the same time, he pioneered the private consulting laboratory, set up at number 103 Milk Street in Boston, Massachusetts, in 1886. In accordance with his will, after his death in 1935 the firm of Arthur D. Little was bequeathed to MIT, where he had studied chemistry and where the firm still does business, conducting, in the words of his original prospectus, "investigations for the improvement of processes and the perfection of products."

In due time, the gospel of research was received at large by American industry. The pioneer industrial research laboratory was founded by General Electric in 1900, for the purpose of investigating all the various applications of electricity. After this, the Du Pont laboratories appeared in 1911, the Kodak Research Laboratories in 1912, followed by laboratories for the United States Rubber Company in 1913, for Standard Oil of New Jersey in 1919, and for the Bell Telephone Company in 1925. By mid-century, the nation had two hundred large industrial research laboratories and at least two thousand others. Besides the research departments of industrial firms there were the government laboratories pioneered by the Department of Agriculture and those in the Department of Commerce established by the Bureau of Standards. By 1988, the combined investment by the federal government and private industry in research amounted to $126 billion. In 1920 (which is as far back as figures can be traced) the amount was only $80 million. The difference is a measure of the impact of what historians call the research revolution.

The Romance of Radio

Magazine science fiction began as a response to the research revolution, to the romance of industrial research. The romance is a bit faded now, but in the early days, when research was a new gospel to be missionized, its spirit was quite literally electrifying. Out of General Electric's investigations into all the various applications of electricity came RCA, the Radio Corporation of America, formed in 1929. From a toy, radio had by the 1920s become a household appliance in all mature industrial nations. "Radio" was once a magic word. It lent glamour even to the movies, with the formation in 1928 of RKO Radio Pictures. Its monument is seventy stories of the RCA building in Rockefeller Center, built during the 1930s, part of a complex of five buildings named Radio City and renowned to all the world for its Radio City Music Hall—now become a relic to be saved by nostalgia buffs.

Science fiction was thus a response to the romance of radio, for Hugo Gernsback evolved *Amazing Stories* out of an earlier series of magazines, starting in 1908 with *Modern Electrics*, the world's first radio magazine. This served as the advertising arm of his radio store, also the world's first, which sold wireless parts to amateurs. He also broadcast programs on station WRNY (326 meters) so the amateurs would have something to listen to (this before KDKA in Pittsburgh began broadcasting on 16 July 1920). Gernsback acted as business manager to the Wireless Association of America during the term of its first president, Lee De Forest, inventor of the vacuum tube that made radio possible.

In 1914 *Modern Electrics* became the *Electrical Experimenter*, which in 1920 became *Science and Invention*, the ancestor of *Popular Science*, "America's favorite what's new magazine" as the ad goes.

It is a joke among science fiction writers that in the early days of *Amazing* they could not get published unless they dreamed up at least three patentable inventions per story. To make sure of that, Gernsback had the stories vetted by his associate editor, Dr. T. O'Conner Sloane, Edison's aging son-in-law. Gernsback himself set the pace with his novel, serialized during 1911 in *Modern Electrics*, entitled *Ralph 124C41+: A Romance of the Year 2660*. Ralph is no Frank Reade, boy wizard; he is the owner of a one-man consulting laboratory, an Arthur D. Little of 2660 A.D. Ralph's perfected products include fluorescent lights, automatic packaging, plastics, radar, jukeboxes, liquid fertilizer, tape recorders, stainless steel, loudspeakers, television (the word is Hugo's coinage), microfilm, vending machines that dispense hot and cold foods and liquids, solar power units, spun glass, a synthetic fiber like nylon for wearing apparel, and spaceships. All of these fantasies and many others now exist, in the twentieth century, and were made possible by industrial research, or what its practitioners call the R & D business.

"R & D" stands for "Research and Development"—scientific research and engineering development. The phrase is doubly significant. The rise of the engineering profession owes as much to big science as the rise of science does to its industrial applications. R & D did not begin in America, however, but it got its name here, famed in the acronym of the RAND Corporation.

The R & D business originated in late nineteenth-century Germany with the application of coal tar chemistry to the manufacture of aniline dyes, and culminated in the formation of the Kaiser Wilhelm Institutes in 1911. That is the great monument to German industrial research—the Kaiser Wilhelm Institutes, a government-led research academy. How else elevate coal tar chemistry? By creating an Aniline City Music Hall?

At all events, supremacy in the R & D business passed to the Americans with the establishment of the General Electric labs, which then set the standard for industrial research laboratories all over the world. And in just about the same year the Kaiser Wilhelm Institutes were formed, R & D found its name in a small company called AMRAD, short for American Radio, and at the same time an acronym for American Research and Development Corporation. AMRAD was a venture of J. P. Morgan, founded and run by a man who had been the wireless operator on Morgan's yacht. It made radio apparatus for amateurs, and it supplied parts for Hugo Gernsback's radio store on 69 West Broadway in New York City. R & D got its name, as did science fiction its impulse, from the radio business.

The Mad Scientist

The novel factor in the R & D equation is industrial science. Industry had always been a practical matter, whereas—until the advent of the research revolution—science dealt with abstract matters and, indeed, was allied with philosophy; scientists studied the world but did not as yet help determine the world. With the industrialization of science, theoretical and practical men assisted each other, brought together in marriage by corporate enterprise or by government. Until then, scientists were to be found only as modestly paid professionals in the university, where they came to roost after the Civil War. Many family fortunes that had supported nonprofessional science were destroyed in the Civil War. Before that, going back to colonial times, the scientist was a wealthy hobbyist, like Benjamin Franklin in silk hose and knee britches, who financed experiments out of pocket for the general good.

The figure of the mad scientist, Dr. Frankenstein of the horror movies, preserves a garbled memory of the elegant amateur whose original civic-mindedness has been forgotten. In Mary Shelley's novel, Dr. Frankenstein is sane enough; he scraps the prototype of his female monster following a vision of her awful offspring. He is remembered as mad probably because he bought his own test tubes. But that is what all nonprofessionals had to do, whether in Pennsylvania or Translyvania, before science was industrialized by the research revolution.

Today, Dr. Frankenstein's commanding genius would make him a great scientific mandarin presiding over group research, like Edwin Land, founder and head of the Polaroid Corporation.[1]

The Rise of "Social" Science Fiction

Science fiction began as a publisher's category in the American pulp magazine industry. Only three magazines devoted exclusively to science fiction still exist, but as a commercial genre science fiction now flourishes more than ever and in a bigger and more profitable market. Every major publishing house has its specialty editor for books on its science fiction list, and quite a number of smaller houses publish only in this one field. Very little of what appears today would be recognized by Hugo Gernsback as belonging to the type of fiction he categorized for *Amazing Stories*. For him, science fiction was meant to glamorize laboratory research and new product design. The progress of industrial science and programmed innovation was his theme—and remains the central theme in what is called the school of "hard core" science fiction. Here, the R & D mystique of old is carried forward undiminished.

But in time a countertheme developed, antiprogressive in tone, that weighed the social costs of applied science against its benefits; here, technology becomes a metaphor, an abstraction for all that is oppressive and dominating in modern society. These two themes, however, equalize each other, in that both are ideological responses to the research revolution, the one finding it uplifting and the other dehumanizing. Apart from the "for technology" and "against technology" forms of science fiction exists another form that could be described as neutral to technology; I group works in this neutral category under the rubric of "social" science fiction.[2] All of these forms coexist in contemporary science fiction, although the evolutionary sequence is as indicated.

Let me offer a simplistic example that demonstrates the evolution of American science fiction. In effect, the genre began with stories about carpenters who rejoiced in their fine tools and then soured on their handiwork, only to blame the tools (runaway robots are endemic embodiments of this latter theme). Then came stories about the carpenters themselves, with questions concerning good or bad hardware (technology) put aside for issues of man and society. For example, if Robert Heinlein's 1940 story, "The Roads Must

Roll," had been done in the Gernsbackian manner, its futuristic transport system—the rolling roads—would have been treated to a loving explanation of its wonders in every technical detail (and maybe with a diagram as well!). A technophobic version, on the other hand, would feature noise pollution or other undesirable side effects. But in the way Heinlein wrote it, the story is really about a labor problem and the question of public duty among the system's maintenance engineers. The mechanical roads are neither displayed as an agent of progress nor introduced to demonstrate the reverse—they are merely assumed. This method is typical of "social" science fiction; a futuristic technology figures only as traditional furniture, neither a glory nor a problem. As a character in the Heinlein story says, "No, it's not the machines, it's the men."

Yet, in some instances, this latest stage in the evolution of science fiction is not at all free of the old R & D ambience. Here, the idea of programmed innovation is applied to the changing and improvement of human society as a whole, not just to its material culture. A scientific study of human needs leads to a planned development for their satisfaction, once they are understood. It becomes a question of cultural engineering, or social R & D. If one hears an echo of scientific or technocratic socialism, one is not mistaken. Actually, stories of this kind predate magazine science fiction. Edward Bellamy's *Looking Backward*, which offers a vision of a technocratic utopia, was published in 1888. But Gernsback and the writers he recruited for *Amazing Stories* were quite innocent of the socialist tradition behind two of the very authors he held up as examples of what he wanted in his magazine.

In his first editorial, he called for "the Jules Verne, H. G. Wells, and Edgar Allan Poe type of story—a charming romance intermingled with scientific fact and prophetic vision." He then proceeded to fill the magazine with reprints from these authors, and waited for the response—readers turned writers for his readers. At that time, no professional science fiction writers were available, apart from numberless hacks who worked within all genres indifferently.

In the previous century, and on into the twentieth, there had been some professional authors who, as part of their output, did write science fiction (it can be called that now, in retrospect), but this work was never regarded by them or by the public as anything other than a component of general fiction. In the United States, it was published in general circulation magazines by such authors as Poe, Hawthorne, and Twain, and in Great Britain, by authors such as H. G. Wells, Rudyard Kipling, and Conan Doyle.

It was up to Gernsback, an electrical engineer, to identify science fiction as a genre written for a special interest readership. Of his three exemplars, it is difficult to know what he saw in Poe that fitted in with his editorial policy. In the event, he did not attract, or publish, any Poe-type stories at all. Poe's feverish romantic imagination was more suited to *Weird Tales*, an earlier fantasy pulp, in which H. P. Lovecraft and Ray Bradbury later made their reputations.

The Misreading of Jules Verne

Jules Verne seems a more obvious choice as a model, with his how-things-work approach to Captain Nemo's *Nautilus*, Robur's flying machine *The Terror*, and the Baltimore Gun Club's *Columbiad*, a space cannon. Indeed, Verne's brand of science fiction inspired a fellow Frenchman to write the very same kind of popular science and popular mechanics that Gernsback himself had published in *Science and Invention* and its predecessors. This one-man industry was Raoul Marquis. Himself an aeronaut, Marquis wrote about balloons (the subject of Verne's first novel and others), all fields of science, however esoteric, and about utilitarian matters as well in his how-to manuals like *L'automobile actuelle en 20 leçons* (The modern motor car in 20 lessons). His list of publications, beginning in the 1880s, fill up twenty-four pages in the printed index to the Bibliotèque Nationale—one measure of his immense popularity,[3] every bit of it riding the wave of Verne's fame. Gernsback, a native of Luxembourg (b. 1884) who emigrated to the United States in 1904, could not have missed Marguis's work and no doubt kept up with it thereafter for ideas to put into his nonfiction magazines.

What Gernsback totally overlooked, however, as did his writers, was that Verne's technical matter was external to the political point of his novels. If Marquis had vulgarized the material in his articles and manuals, so too had Gernsback in deciding upon the contents of *Amazing Stories*. Thus did American science fiction get underway as a response to the research industry and its programmed invention, the lone inventor (like Captain Nemo or Robur) updated with figures modeled after Arthur D. Little, a consulting scientist and engineer just as Sherlock Holmes was a consulting detective. Soon after, team research was introduced by John W. Campbell (an early writer for *Amazing* who later became the field's greatest editor when he took over *Astounding Science Fiction* in 1937) with the corporation-based scientists of his "Arcot, Morey and Wade" series.

But even to this day, Verne is completely misunderstood. Very much the political writer, his ideological matter, when it got too explicit, was edited out of the standard English translations (fully one-third of *Twenty Thousand Leagues under the Sea* is excised). These expurgations were made mainly by a conservative British cleric, who was ignorant of science and technology to such an extent that he mistranslated, confused, and generally butchered their details in whatever parts he left intact.[4] Thus Verne was presented to the readers of *Amazing Stories* (where he was reprinted in these awful translations) as a writer of juvenile invention stories, and as a Frenchman impatient with detailed research who made a lot of mistakes—but never mind, American writers would improve on that! Thus Verne's reputation in the English-speaking world is as a writer both childish and careless, although European readers know him as an adult writer who used his *voyages extraordinaires* to dramatize his brand of socialism, authenticating them with a technical precision of stupefying mastery. Gernsback surely was familiar with Verne in the original French, yet he failed as badly as did Marquis to get the ideological message.

The key biographical fact for an understanding of Verne's work is his induction, at the height of his fame, into the French Legion of Honor by none other than Ferdinand de Lesseps, builder of the Suez Canal and a disciple of Henri Saint-Simon. Saint-Simon is the pre-Marxist patriarch of socialism, whose first disciple and secretary, Auguste Comte (the father of positivism), coined the word *socialism*, and the word *sociology* as well (a new "positive" or natural science needed for research into human society the better to change and improve it with socialism). What Comte meant by socialism is technocratic socialism. The Saint-Simonians worshiped industrial production as a worldwide process, instead of the international proletarian worker as in later Marxism, and their slogan was, "The whole world belongs to mankind."

Their romantic globalism is captured in Verne's most famous novel, *Around the World in Eighty Days*. As apostles of world transport and a world-industrial civilization, their program was in part fulfilled by the huge contribution of de Lesseps.

The Saint-Simonians held that the industrial revolution would make for a socialist (or technocratic) revolution, replacing the feudal love of war with peaceful production, and the superstitions of religion with science. Not being anticapitalist, class-war socialists like the Marxists, the aim of their revolution was to unite all mankind in universal association for the exploitation of nature, thus to end for all time the exploitation of man by man—mankind divided by warfare.

Verne's great novelization of this doctrinal thesis is *From the Earth to the Moon* (1865), drafted during the fourth year of the American Civil War. As a Saint-Simonian socialist, Verne pondered American wartime technology, and wondered how it might be converted to peacetime industry. He wondered how to redirect such destructive energies for a creative project? His answer, as

the war concluded, was to symbolically melt down its entire arsenal of can-
nons for the casting of the *Columbiad*, to be used for the development of in-
terplanetary travel and the peaceful colonization of space. But the moonshot
is not America's project alone.

The Baltimore Gun Club that initiates the project raises funds for it from a
worldwide subscription drive. All humanity is drawn into the plan with collective enthusiasm. The Gun Club itself is internationalized on the model of
the Council of Newton, the name Saint-Simon gave the brain center of his
world directorate. It calls upon scientific talent wherever it is to be found,
including the world's astronomers to track the moon capsule in flight.
Moreover, the Gun Club wins to its purpose the happy collaboration of the
American workforce, organized on a gigantic scale as one single workshop. In
its exalted atmosphere of class collaboration between captains of industry
and proletarian workers, all of this in the service of man's harmonious conquest of nature, Verne's novel is a technocratic hymn to the partnership of
knowledge and work, science and labor. The arts of war are indeed translated
into peaceful production.

The submarine *Nautilus*, in *Twenty Thousand Leagues under the Sea*, is
also a miniature Saint-Simonian world. Captain Nemo directs a crew of international sailors who speak a synthetic language, something like Esperanto.
Their work, however, is not peaceful production; it is making war for peace,
the sinking of British ships by way of punishing the imperial homeland for its
colonial wars. In this mission, Captain Nemo is not unlike the hero of *Robur
the Conqueror* and *Master of the World*. Robur and his international crew
smite the world's warships from out of the sky with their bomb-laden aircraft, *The Terror*, enforcing upon all nations a unity of cooperative oneness in
the "economic and political ways of the world." For the whole world, indeed,
the whole universe, belongs to mankind.[5]

Overlooking the Ideology of H. G. Wells

All of this was missed by Gernsback, as was the fact that his third example, H. G. Wells, was also a socialist writer in the same Saint-Simonian tradition. This is made evident in Wells's 1936 film, *Things to Come*, still
taken by science fiction fans to be no more than a prophecy of space
travel—except for that dumb mistake about the Space Gun. But what else
is it, if not another version of the story of *Columbiad*, with all the political
symbolism it implies? And leading on to its trial firing is a war to end war, a
war for peace under the leadership of John Cabal, another Robur with his
cosmopolitan League of the Airmen. Imposing its *pax aeronautica* upon

the shattered sovereignties of a great international conflict, which it ended by entering to deliver the knockout blow, John Cabal establishes a temporary world government, the Air Dictatorship. This passes on for consolidation to his grandson, Oswald Cabal, the Newtonian president of a technocratic World Council of Direction—he who fires the Space Gun, at film's end, in the name of a united humanity.[6]

The early Wellsian novels of science fiction that Gernsback reprinted are no less ideological, providing a means "to discuss sociology [read "socialism"] in fable" as Wells himself said of them.[7] But the editorial policy of *Amazing Stories* was to say of them, in effect, "No, it's not the men, it's the machines" that matter. This bias was highlighted in the artwork. For example, the full-page interior illustration for *The Time Machine* features the machine itself, in its futuristic setting, with all the elaborate detail of a diagram from *The Electrical Experimenter*, with the imagined electrics given the most attention. The fannish writers who picked up on this, in their own stories about time travel, focused on the same engineering aspect; where the machines went was but an excuse for shoptalk about how they worked. Small wonder that Wells came to hate the very name of "science fiction" as applied to his work, as he looked back with scorn on this fictionalized electrotechnical journal in which his first and most famous novel had reappeared for all the wrong reasons.[8]

Or again, take *The War of the Worlds*. This work was turned into a cover story, with the Martian fighting machines emblazoned in full color, their operating details worked out to the last functional degree, followed by stories of Martian technology. Or yet again, the industrial machinery of the Selenites in *The First Men in the Moon* was illustrated with a minuteness of care for particulars that nowhere are described in the novel, for the story itself is really about the utopian triumph of a Saint-Simonian technocracy in its organizational details. Pictured as a society occupying the interior of an entire planetoid, it is a prophecy of things to come on Earth, when mankind will be "united in one brotherhood" as a global species, like the Selenites under their brainy Grand Lunar; what is coming is a single terrestrial workshop governed by some Newtonian world dictator to the ends of peaceful production.

Trained as a biologist, Wells added to the collective aspect of his technocratic socialism the element of Darwinism, insofar as he stressed that the basic unit of mankind is not the individual or even a particular human culture, but the species. And if Man is a global species, unified at the biological level, anything partisan or particular, like social classes or nation states, must go against his true interests, which are to match up the biological with the social and the political on a worldwide basis. This truth about human destiny—ignored by the class-war socialism of Karl Marx—is the hidden message of *The Time*

Machine. The Time Traveller visits the future only to find that the social divisions of the present order, as between workers and the owning class, have not in the least been overcome by a proletarian attempt at insurgency. In fact, class warfare has led to such an increase in the social distance between its two parties that they have become two different species, the Eloi and the Morlocks. Thus the small-scale social tragedy of the unfortunate workers is not to be resolved by class action, but by human concerns on a larger scale, involving the fate of all mankind. This is good Saint-Simonian doctrine, class collaboration in a world industrial civilization, admixed with biological reductionism.

Such are the socialist and Darwinian themes of "social" science fiction, as treated by many of today's genre writers, among them Harry Harrison. Ironically, this latest development in American science fiction returns it to the main exemplars of its first stage, Jules Verne and H. G. Wells, none of whose contemporaries understood their meaning, as most readers and would-be imitators still do not. Harry Harrison, for one, does.

Harrison and the Great American Adventure Story

Harrison earned his fame in *Astounding Science Fiction* (ASF), edited by his idol, John W. Campbell. The Campbell years of this magazine are noted for bringing forth what are today the greatest names in modern science fiction. Needless to say, the authors in question brought to the genre a maturity of style and content far removed from the primitive stage of Gernsbackian, technophilic science fiction.

But ASF began life in January 1930 as an action-adventure pulp magazine titled *Astounding Stories of Super Science*, where the "science" was marginal at best; it was just a new way of marketing melodramatic adventure stories. The cover art on the first issue suggests the editorial policy. An aviator in leather flying togs and goggled helmet is engaged in fisticuffs with a giant beetle with many-colored spots on its carapace; the fight takes place in some alien landscape, far, far away in another galaxy, as we may suppose. How the aviator got there in the kind of vehicle his dress indicates is truly a marvel of super science.

This is rather less genre science fiction than it is a hoked-up, dumbed-down epigone of the main current of mainstream American fiction. According to Martin Green in *The Great American Adventure* (1984), the action stories of America's best adventure writers (he surveys Cooper, Dana, Irving, Melville, Twain, Hemingway, Faulkner, and Mailer, among others) lie at the heart of the native tradition. The adventure story is *the* great genre of American letters, the true genre of the American experience.

Where does Harry Harrison stand within the science fiction genre? He belongs to its latest and most mature phase, that of social science fiction. But at the same time he reverts to the earliest, technophilic phase with his unabashed love of science and technology. He is a writer given to criticizing his fellows in the field for not doing their scientific homework, and who delights in speaking of "Machine as Hero."[9]

This mix of technophilic with social science fiction may seem to be a contradiction, but it is resolved through the narrative format he chose for all thirty-five of his novels, comic or serious: the action story. He thus harks back to the heroics of super science, only with the science restored, and with an appreciation of the literary sources from which degenerated that aviator in combat with the beetle.

Through his work, Harrison has carved out for himself a unique place in the genre of science fiction, as the vigorous writer of intelligent adventure stories. His immense popularity is due, no doubt, to the fact that he successfully has tapped into the main genre of traditional American letters.

Chapter Two

The Man Whose Pen Name
Is His Real Name

Spring 1956. New York City. A low-rent, walk-up apartment building on West 15th Street. It is either very late at night or very early in the morning. I hear a bunch of singing rowdies, pounding their way up the cast-iron staircase. They sound like drunken sailors. As a graduate student just newly moved in and already burning the mid-night oil, I open the door and step out. They *are* drunken sailors, or at least tipsy sailors. But they are not American sailors.

Reaching my floor, they ask for directions in a language I do not know. One of them shows me a smeared address on a wrinkled shred of paper. I point across the hallway. But before one of them can raise a knuckle to knock, the opposite door opens and a man sporting a black moustache and goatee and black horn-rimmed glasses hustles them inside, shushing them in their language to be quiet.

I step out into the hallway again when I hear them reemerge, to see them quizzically consulting each other about the little booklets that look like passports that they now hold in their hands. They *are* passports, and they are not illegal forgeries, nothing conspiratorial was done, the shushing was to keep the sailors from waking the baby, and the man was Harry Harrison—today white-haired and wearing even blacker horn-rimmed glasses.

That was my first meeting with Harry Harrison, a friend of such long standing that it is awkward to refer to him as Harrison as required by the editorial formalities of this series. With the mystery of the sailors cleared up in a jiffy, it was only moments before we discovered our mutual interest in science fiction. Not long after we set about planning to edit the first theme anthology in science fiction, which eventually appeared in 1968 as *Apeman, Spaceman: Anthropological Science Fiction*. It took more than a dozen years to see print, but working at it now and again kept us in touch.

As for the sailors, two words suffice to explain everything—the name "Gary Davis", although younger readers will need the help of a historical footnote here. Gary Davis, the son of Meyer Davis the millionaire bandleader, was the original peacenik. He had been a bomber pilot during World

War II, but when the United Nations (as the Allies were called) met in Paris on 10 February 1947 to sign a peace treaty with the Axis powers in Europe, Gary Davis stood on the photogenic steps of the Palais de Chaillot and burned his American passport, and declared himself a world citizen. This was flashworthy news. Gary Davis launched a global movement, and set up branches everywhere; the biggest ones even had their own newspapers. Unfortunately, the whole thing eventually got bigger than he could handle; he was not the organizing type and was done in by the inevitable power struggles from within that ensued. Until such time as he got kicked out of the movement, he maintained an office at 222 Park Avenue, supporting himself and adding to his fame by starring in the road company of *Stalag 17*.

Harrison met him at the Hydra Club, to which somebody had brought him as a guest. The Hydra Club was organized in New York City in 1947 by Frederik Pohl, Lester del Rey, Judith Merrill, William Tenn (pen name of Phil Klass), David Kyle, "Doc" Lowndes, and four others (nine in all, hence the name Hydra, after the number of heads that had organized it) as a fan club for science fiction professionals and their friends. Harrison joined as a friend, before he enjoyed membership as a fellow professional.

The sailors had been sent to the Harrison apartment by Gary Davis, who had a way of persuading all sorts of new people he met to apply for his curious world passports, whether they needed one or not. Strange as it may seem, these irregular documents actually proved useful (given that customs officials did not always examine them too closely) in helping more than a few stateless persons to make the international moves of their choice. It was to serve that end that Harrison had designed the passports and stored a carton of them at 15th Street, ready to disburse them at almost any hour, an act of hospitality not unconnected with his doings in the Esperanto Movement.

By the time I met Gary Davis he was undergoing therapy with an Indian guru. Shattered now by the warring factions of the peace movement, he was given up by nearly all his friends but Harrison, whose personal loyalties, once formed, are unshakable. Moreover, Harrison much appreciated and never forgot the "emotional statement" Gary Davis made on the steps of the Palais de Chaillot.

Soon the Harrisons, with baby Todd, were to depart for Mexico, as Gary Davis left for France on the Ile de France. Only he never got there. He became the man without a country because he had burned his U.S. passport, and so was shuttled back and forth across the Atlantic until he escaped into Italy, where his life again intersected with Harrison's.

Beginnings

Harry Harrison was born Henry Maxwell Dempsey on 12 March 1925 in Stamford, Connecticut, the only child of Ria Kirjassoff and Henry (or Hank or Harry) Dempsey. When he was two years old, the family moved to Brooklyn, and a few years later to Queens, where he grew up.

Henry Dempsey was Irish with an Irish sense of humor that was not lost on his son. By trade a printer, the father was a top technologist in his field, consulted by other experts for the final degree of expertise. But during the Depression he found little employment on his own as a substitute proof-reader and compositor on the New York *Daily News*. He worked only if a regular printer called in sick, which meant that he worked just one night a week or every two weeks—not enough to pay the rent. Hence a hectic re-moval from one apartment to another every two or three months or so (as long as the credit lasted), with furniture moved at night in a friendly iceman's cart. Harry Harrison jokes that perhaps he got his peripatetic hab-its from this experience; but there can be no doubt where his own skill as a printer comes from. He started learning on a small printing press with a chase, or metal form, three by five inches in size, used for making up busi-ness cards and postcards, that his father had brought home for him to play with when still a preschooler.

His mother left Czarist Russia at age fifteen and was a grade school teacher until she married. Indeed, she is descended from a family of teachers and rab-bis. Harrison attributes his didactic turn of mind to her influence, although she ran no orthodox household. His parents took a *laissez-faire* attitude to-ward religion, and let Harry pick his own faith for himself. It turned out to be scientific humanism (which he invariably capitalizes, Scientific Humanism, in his didactic fiction).

It is worth pausing a moment to consider this doctrine because, as Harrison says, he perceived science fiction to be an atheistic literature even be-fore he discovered scientific humanism. The term was first introduced by Walter Lippman in his *Preface to Morals* (1929) to denote a philosophical at-titude based upon science and morals without religion; its argument is to show that ethics can be derived from scientific knowledge. In America, its most notable exponent was the philosopher and educator Max Otto, who popularized it in a chapter called "Scientific Humanism" in his mass paper-back book of 1949, *Science and the Moral Life*. Interviewing Harrison, I found that he faithfully articulated the doctrine as given in these sources. I asked, "Do you mean all this boils down to BOMFOG without the FOG?" "Yes," he said, getting the rather irreverent, acronymic allusion to that standard pietism, the Brotherhood of Man under the Fatherhood of God. "Yes; the Brotherhood of Man minus the Fatherhood of God." With no hope of help from God, and no faith in life immortal, the beauty and love of human comradeship is all the more precious. A fraternal world community is therefore all the more compelling as a morally corrective ideal.[1] (Perhaps this is more precisely a sentimental than a scientific humanism, better named humanitarian idealism.)

Like many writers, Harrison was a precocious reader (from age five), although the ambition to write was not formed so early. He did, however, discover science fiction at age seven through an 1932 issue of *Amazing Stories*. Later he ran across the *Astounding Science Fiction* of John W. Campbell and found its editorial policy "wired directly to my brain." But he also read some of the other pulp genres: war, air war, railroad stories, hero-centered pulps like *Doc Savage* and *Operator 5*, but no detective fiction or westerns. More serious reading he borrowed from the Queens Borough Public Library at the rate of ten or twenty books a week. There he discovered the nautical novels of C. S. Forester, which he studied for their economy of style and clarity of technical exposition. In all, he was quite a bookish boy, given to solitude, as well he might be in view of all the changes of school that shifting addresses necessitated. He did not make his first real friend among his classmates until he was twelve. Shy and introspective by nature or long habit, the outgoing personality of today, as part of his business, is a product of will. "I'm a trained extrovert," he says, with an amused hint of the paradoxical about it.

Changing schools all the time did not help his grades, but he always managed to do well in English and science. He was interested in the school magazine or paper wherever he attended, but it was drawing, not writing, that he contributed.

At age thirteen he did something more to the purpose of his true calling when it finally revealed itself. Newly friends with some peers for the first time in his life, he joined with a group of them as charter members of the Queens chapter of the Science Fiction League. The Science Fiction League was launched in 1934 by Hugo Gernsback with the aid of Charles D. Horning, the young fannish editor of *Wonder Stories* in whose pages the club's activities were mainly reported and suggested. The first and most successful effort at organized fandom, the Science Fiction League was not long in forming local chapters throughout the United States, Britain, and elsewhere. It provided the lasting basis, not only for the many regional science fiction conventions of today, but for those Worldcons at which the Hugo Awards have been bestowed from 1953.[2]

I have before me as I write a copy of the by-laws of the Queens Science Fiction League, ratified and signed on Sunday, 6 November 1938. That was the year in which the first American regional convention was held in New York City, and where the following year the premier Worldcon was held. Article 2 of the by-laws pledges the members, among other things, to attend that great event: "The purpose of the Queens Science Fiction League shall be to popularize science fiction locally; to discuss and criticize current science fiction literature; to publish a club magazine; to conduct scientific experiments along lines suggested in science fiction stories; to make an amateur scientifilm; and to participate in the World Science Fiction Convention as the official New York representative of New Fandom."

Of the fourteen members who signed only one other, aside from Harrison, made a career of science fiction: Sam Moskowitz. A nonacademic historian of the genre and an indefatigable anthologist, he is the number one authority on the history of early science fiction fandom, recounted in his first book, *The Immortal Storm* (1954). It certainly is his most memorable title, and it shows how seriously he takes the feuds of the late 1930s among what was then a tiny group of science fiction fans, who debated the relative merits of their favorite authors and stories with a heat that was indeed quite intense.[3]

Attending Forest Hills High School in Queens, Harrison, bookish as ever, was head of its "library squad," students who worked at classification and shelving. At graduation in 1943, he was tagged in the school yearbook as "glider Harrison" for his hobby of building model planes and gliders, and for his plans to build a real glider and fly in it. But 1943 was the middle of World War II; boys who graduated that year belonged to the "no hope" class because they were fated only to be drafted into the armed services.

Military Service and Higher Education

Two months after graduation Harrison was drafted, but into the service of his choice, the U.S. Army Air Corps. He had arranged that by attending Eastern Aircraft Instrument School in Jersey City, New Jersey, a U.S. government approved instrument repair station, and becoming certified, with good to excellent ratings, as an aircraft instrument mechanic. He never again saw a centrifugal tachometer or Bourdon tube pressure gauge. The Air Corps, having tested him as tops in mechanical aptitude (not to say in general intelligence), sent Harrison to Lowry Field in Denver, Colorado, for some very sophisticated technical training in something else. There he was designated as a 678-3, the code number for the highest ranking technical skill in that service (he held the rank of private throughout the war, until he was discharged as a sergeant). He was trained to be a power-operated and computing-gunsight specialist, and worked with the Sperry Mark 1 computer. This at the time was a secret device, the very same secret behind the Norden Bombsight his fellows on base were trained to use. He learned computer theory and how to repair the Sperry, a preelectronic device of miniature rods and cogs, under clean room conditions.

In 1944 he was sent to an Air Corps base in Laredo, Texas, where gunners were taught, from power-turrets mounted on trucks, how to fire a pair of computer-aimed, fifty-caliber machine guns. His job was to repair and service the Sperry in his unit, but soon he was doing four jobs in one, as first the truck driver, then the armorer, and then the gunnery instructor, when each was successively called away to combat duty, leaving only the indispensable technical expert, omnicompetent Pvt. Harrison, serial no. 3295927. Low rank in a high tech job was the order of things in those days.

In the winter of 1945 he was transferred to another gunnery school in Panama City, Florida, which soon after closed down, whereupon he was detailed to M.P. duty and promptly promoted to sergeant. His job this time was "riding shotgun" on a garbage truck, guarding the black prisoners who worked it. They did not require much guarding, Harrison learned after drinking with them in the black servicemen's bar; after landing in the brig, they now wanted only to serve their time with the best of behavior, get an honorable discharge, and so properly stake their claim to the G.I. Bill of Rights.

Sergeant Harrison was discharged on 14 February 1946 with all the standard medals—the American Service Medal, the Good Conduct Medal, the World War II Victory Medal, but the one he really earned, he says, was that of Sharpshooter (between ordinary Marksman and Expert). Although he served his country well, with all the distinction his esoteric training had prepared him for, he left the service with an abiding dislike of military life. But this experience did not go to waste. From it he gained a start on his lifelong interest in computers. From it also he gathered the memories that his imagination transmuted into the comic inferno of military life in *Bill, the Galactic Hero* (1965).

His first civilian move was to attend Hunter College in New York City (just turned coeducational after the war), where he studied under its most notable professor of art, John Blomshield. Blomshield was no mere academic teaching *about* art; he was a practicing painter of distinction, belonging to the Mannerist school (a traditional style of realism, with curiously modern and complex distortions of perspective, dating back to sixteenth-century Europe). Harrison soon quit the small class of eight to study under Blomshield privately for two years, from 1946 to 1948; and his house today has Blomshield paintings hung all about.

At the same time, he enrolled in the Cartoonists and Illustrators School, where he was able from the start to produce saleable work from what he was learning. He sold *Writers Digest* his first article, titled "How to Write for the Comics," although that was not what he was doing. His contracts with the comic book industry instead called for his turning scripts into pictures and balloons, panel by panel. The writers who turned out such scripts would specify, for example, "On page 2, panel 1, Bill kisses Mary (profile), says, 'Oh, oh, oh.' "

From Comic Books to Science Fiction

Having learned the ins and outs of that trade while working at it in art school, Harrison left it to set up his own comic book factory. And factory is the right word, with its industrial division of labor between pencil men, inking men, erasure men, border men, and so on. (In "Portrait of the Artist" he tells an amusing story of technological unemployment in this industry, caused by the automation of its each and every subdivided function.) But he was also doing illustrations for the science fiction magazines, such as *Galaxy* and *Marvel Science Stories*; these gained him membership in the Hydra Club. By 1950, he was chairman of Hydracon, a New York convention organized by Hydra Club professionals but open to the public.

Factory management led to higher things, to real entrepreneurship in the comics industry, as a "packager" (a commercial term for one who designs and manufactures a product or series of related products). Harrison was packaging three comic book titles at a Park Avenue address, in an office shared with Gary Davis. These were a romance (*Girls' Love Stories*), a horror (*Beware*), and an imitation *Mad* comics (*Nuts*). For all three he himself did the cover art, the two-page filler, and, for the romance, a letter column (advice to the lovelorn) signed "Barbara Miles." In one issue of *Nuts* (November 1954) he did the (unsigned) story, "Captain Marble Flies Again." And he was contributing scripts to DC Comics as well, the top company in the field.

In those days, comic books were very big business—650 titles in print with a combined circulation of one hundred million copies per month.[4] But the market crashed in 1955. A congressional investigation into the industry had determined that it was corrupting the youth of the nation. Magazine distributers were scared, and returned what they judged to be the most offensive titles to the publishers. Only about three hundred titles remained on the market after that, none of them the "crappy" ones Harrison depended on (his word). Although he continued to do work in this field, his packaging days were over.

Before that happened, however, Harrison wrote his first science fiction story, "Rock Diver." It reworks a western plot about claim jumpers, using a classic science fiction device, the matter penetrator; still it glints with touches of the Harrison wit his readers have since come to relish. Sick from tonsillitis and racked by hay fever, his hands were so shaky that he could not draw but could type. He was already down in the dumps from the ending of an "unfortunate first marriage";[5] and no doubt his mind and body both were treating each other badly at that point. One of his current jobs was doing illustrations for *Worlds Beyond* (three issues, December 1950–February 1951), edited by Damon Knight, then just beginning an eminent career in American science fiction writing and editing. When Harrison asked Damon Knight for advice on how to sell the story, Knight responded by taking it himself, just in time for what turned out to be the last issue of *Worlds Beyond*. From then on, Harrison turned to the services of a literary agent, his first one being Frederik Pohl, before he made his name as a writer. Pohl then was handling more science fiction magazine and book contracts than all other agencies combined.[6]

Soon after Harrison got his personal life settled once and for all, when on 4 June he married Joan Merkler. She was a dress designer and ballet dancer whom he met through a mutual friend, a jewelry designer he shared a studio with after Gary Davis decamped his Park Avenue office. As I recall from a long ago visit there, it was a pretty shabby little walkup studio, rotting wooden stairs and all, some undisturbed relic of underdevelopment in the very shadows of Radio City. Joan's parents, from the upper echelons of the New York garment industry, were not wildly enthusiastic about the marriage. But she rightly saw in him the man he was and stuck by him, traveled the world with him (thirty-two countries), learned five or six of its languages with him, cooked its various foods for him, guarded his career like a gryphon and raised their two children, Todd and Moira.

Harrison did not want to continue in the comics industry, but it did sustain him while he pursued his interest in science fiction at little or no pay, before he made his own opportunities in this field. Then on Harrison's advice four different science fiction comics were inaugurated: *Weird Fantasy* (1950–53), *Weird Science* (1950–53), *Weird Science-Fantasy* (1954–55), and *Incredible Science Fiction* (1955–56). Despite their horrific titles, these were the most sophisticated science fiction comics to have appeared to that point, illustrated by well-known science fiction artists, with story adaptations from authors as important as Ray Bradbury.[7] But these, too, disappeared with the advent of the 1955 Comics Code that followed the congressional investigations.

Harrison also served as editor on a number of minor and short-lived science fiction magazines. Working for Space Publications, he edited *Rocket Stories* (April, July, September 1953), *Space Science Fiction* (eight issues: May 1952–September 1953), and *Science Fiction Adventures* (nine issues: November 1952–June 1954). He also worked on *Fantasy Magazine* (February, June, August, November 1953).[8] (As late as 1968–69, he took over at *Amazing Stories* when it was troubled and otherwise editorless.)

Naturally, this work was not enough to occupy fully a man like Harrison. He also took up a position as art director for the ten magazines of publisher John Raymond. Among his titles was a rival to *Ebony* called *Brown*, for which Harry did all the layouts and production work. For the others, unknown to the publisher, he also wrote a good deal of their copy under a variety of pen names. Allowed to start his own magazine, a pulp, under this publisher's imprint, Harry founded *Sea Stories* (borrowed from an original title of the 1920s). It lasted only one issue, but he had done everything in it and on it— the cover art, the interior art, the filler, the letters (where were they supposed to come from, with no previous issues?), and most of the stories (under more pen names).

With that kind of on-the-job training, hack writing for a captive market, Harrison decided to go free lance, to write anything anybody would buy, at whatever the traffic would bear. He soon found out that the best markets were men's adventure magazines and women's confession magazines. They paid ten cents a word, ten times more than the best paying science fiction magazines. Among his favorite titles from that awful era are "I Went Down with My Ship" and "My Iron Lung Baby."[9]

While he was doing this free-lance writing, he was able to save most of his earnings by working as art director of *Pic* and *Picture Week* after asking Bruce Elliot for the job. Elliott had written commissioned stories for Harrison when he was editing and needed help. Now Elliott, managing editor of these and other dime pocket magazines, returned the favor, offering the choice of art director or copy editor. Harrison wanted the former job so that he could do graphic design and layout all day, sparing his writing energies for his evenings. He hoped to make and save enough money so that he could afford to write for *Astounding Science Fiction* (ASF), which only paid two cents a word.

Free-Lance Traveler

The Harrisons had been married now—it is 1956—for two years, and baby Todd, born 21 May 1955, was just a little more than one year old. Come summertime they simply cleared out, packing baby Todd and a load of necessities into an old Ford and heading for a quiet place with a pleasant climate in rural Mexico. There in Cuautla, a small market town almost sixty miles south of Mexico City, Harrison began work on *Deathworld*, his first novel.

The following year the Harrisons moved to London, taking advantage of a cheap fan flight to the first Worldcon to be held outside the United States. While in London, Harry continued work on *Deathworld* and initiated correspondence about it with John W. Campbell, the editor of ASF to whom he hoped to sell the novel and a man—as writer and editor—he had long admired from afar.

At this point it is essential to insert something about this man, whom Harrison came to know and love deeply. John W. Campbell (1910–71) brought magazine science fiction out of its primitive, Gernsbackian beginnings. Starting in *Amazing Stories* in 1930, he quickly became one of the most popular masters of the super-science story (second only to E. E. Smith), moving on under the name of Don A. Stuart to write stories of such a different and influential kind that they are regarded as forming the very keystone of modern science fiction. He became editor of *Astounding Stories* in 1947, then changed the title to *Astounding Science Fiction* (later to *Analog Science Fiction/Science Fact*), and soon developed the writers who were to become the mainstays of the genre.

Among those to contribute eulogies in *Locus* ("The newspaper of the science fiction field") was Harry Harrison, who wrote:

> John Campbell was the single greatest editor in this field, you all know that, and he was a writer of great merit as well whose early books are still in print. He, singlehandedly, shaped modern science fiction, you know that.
>
> What many readers, who never met him in person, may not know, is that he was a warm and wonderful human being. A friend. A man who was really without malice, who believed in people and mankind.
>
> I am going to miss him very much. This is a very sad time.[10]

An earlier tribute to the living man was the anthology, *John W. Campbell: Collected Editorials from Analog* (1966).[11]

Shortly before Campbell's death, Harrison also managed in 1971 to capture on film his inimitable manner as a working editor, the way he developed story ideas with his authors at his desk or over lunch. This twenty-eight–minute 16mm film, called "Lunch with John Campbell", was produced by Professor James Gunn for the Audio-Visual Center at the University of Kansas, as one in a series of filmed interviews with science fiction writers and editors. [12] In it, Harry Harrison and Gordon Dickson evolve a story idea with the help of Campbell's input, this just for demonstration purposes; but after Campbell died, they wrote it up as the *Analog* serial "Lifeboat," retitled *The Lifeship* (1976) in its book version.

These events prompt one more digression on Harrison's theory of collaboration. He says it should be "synergistic," a dynamic cooperation for enhanced results. His first try at this was our joint novel, *Stonehenge* (1972), revised and expanded as *Stonehenge: Where Atlantis Died* (1983). Since then, he also has learned how to mobilize a whole team of technical advisors as he did for the mammoth *West of Eden* project (see chapter 11).

The Harrisons in January 1958 left England for Italy and the Isle of Capri, after Harry wrote one more—and last—true confession to pay for the trip. He was not drawn to Capri, however, because of its fame in song, but rather because Gary Davis was planning to go there to escape from the Italian police, having no passport other than World Passport No. 1, and he scouted the place for the Harrisons to rent not long before he was arrested. Harrison continued to work on *Deathworld*, partially supporting himself by working with Dan Berry, the American artist now living in France who had sheltered Gary Davis during his unauthorized sojourn there. Berry needed a writer to script the "Flash Gordon" comic strip he was reviving for King Features, and could not think of anyone better than Harrison, the only man in Europe who knew both the cartooning business and science fiction writing. He ended up doing "Flash Gordon" longer than expected, ten long years, from 1958 to 1968, because his crooked agent for the men's magazines had stolen all his earnings from that source after he left New York. But an old friend, Hans Stefan Santesson, came to the rescue. As editor of *Fantastic Universe* (September 1956–March 1960), he would send Harrison a story title from time to time, with payment in advance, each one of which was good for a month of living expenses from only three or four days of work. Harrison developed all these titles as robot stories, collected as *War with the Robots* (1962).

In late 1958 the Harrisons returned to New York City for the prenatal care of their next child, who was born on 9 January 1959 and named Moira. Still trying to finish *Deathworld*, stay alive, and feed his family, he had one reluctant foot in the comics, scripts for "Flash Gordon" and for English science fiction comic magazines he had started working for while in London. (At that time, he had also scripted the science fiction newspaper comic strip, "Jeff Hawke.")

Finally, *Deathworld* appeared as a three-part serial in ASF (January, February, March 1959) and as a book later that year under the Bantam imprint, a paperback original, handled for him by the late agent Robert P. Mills

(Harrison was his first client), editor of *Magazine of Fantasy and Science Fiction* from its inception in 1949 until 1962. Established now with John Campbell, Harrison undertook to write one serial per year for *Analog*, as well as writing science fiction stories for this and other magazines. He now dropped the comics (except the tiresome but needed "Flash Gordon") and the adventure magazines to strive after a living as a full-time science fiction writer—given that he could find the right place to live.

His choice was Denmark. His contact for that part of the world was a Danish painter he overheard in Mexico trying to explain his automobile problems in French to a mechanic; Harrison volunteered to translate, friendship and correspondence followed. The painter, Preben Zahle, also happened to be the art director on *Tidens Kvinder*, the leading Danish woman's magazine, who later took some articles by Harrison for translation, and even a collaboration with Joan Harrison on an article about travelling with children (about which she was an expert). This friend arranged for a pension in Copenhagen in the summer of 1959, where the Harrisons had intended only a visit before moving on they knew not where. But they liked Denmark so much that they stayed there, at various locations, for six years. They were settled at last in Snekkersten, a small fishing village, when I called upon them in August 1964, having travelled halfway around the world, through the whole length of the Soviet Union from Tokyo, Japan, on the Trans-Siberian railroad. At that time Harrison and I chose the final title for our anthology of anthropological science fiction, and at last *Apeman, Spaceman* was published in 1968. Harry had already put together two story collections of his own, *War with the Robots* (1962) and *Two Tales and 8 Tomorrows* (1965), and written the heavily researched ecological novel, *Planet of the Damned* (1962), plus a ghosted title under the name of the mystery writer Leslie Charteris, *Vendetta for the Saint* (1964).

While in Denmark, he also did some rather specialized science journalism for the *Medical Tribune*, partly as a favor to its regular stringer, a neighboring writer who took a year off from it in 1959, and partly to be paid for doing research that would be useful in writing science fiction. He made direct use of his experience in two stories published in 1966. "The Voice of the CWACC" (an acronym pronounced "quack") and "CWACC Strikes Again." The stories deal with a foundation (Committee for Welfare, Administration, and Consumer Control) that funds offbeat medical research when it looks promising, even if (especially if) the proposal is couched in the language of theories repudiated by the American Medical Association—just what CWACC seeks. For ethical reasons, however, he decided not to use the Harry Harrison byline, as with the *Medical Tribune* articles, but a pseudonym adding one more to a long list of pen names and editorial house names. This one was Hank Dempsey. But wait! Isn't Hank Dempsey his *real* name?

What's in a Name?

Now I am ready to break the suspense and unriddle the conundrum built into this chapter title, "The Man Whose Pen Name Is His Real Name." If you have been teased along this far, here is the answer. When Harrison first looked at his birth certificate at age thirty, needing it in order to get a passport for his move to Mexico, he found the name inscribed thereon was Henry [Hank] Maxwell Dempsey. Now his father, Henry or Harry Dempsey, was a Dempsey most of his life; but later on changed his name to Harrison, after the name of his step-father. Son Henry was always called Harry Harrison at home and so his name reads on his grade school diploma; but it is not the name on his birth certificate. Thus Harry Harrison is really a pen name, although the author of "Rock Diver" did not know it at the time. By the time of *Deathworld*, Harry Harrison had become the "real" name of choice, as well as habit, so that his discovery that he was really Hank Dempsey was but an amusing surprise.

When serialized in ASF, *Deathworld* won first place in the readership polls conducted every month by John Campbell in his regular feature, "The An Lab" (short for analytical laboratory). This meant a bonus payment of one cent a word, but more important it signified success in the premier magazine of Harrison's chosen field. He followed it with two top-ranking sequels, "The Ethical Engineer" (July, August 1963) and "The Horse Barbarians" (February, March, April 1968), later retitled in book form as *Deathworld 2* and *Deathworld 3*. The point of getting published with bonus-winning serials in *Analog* was that it gave Harrison recognition as another Campbell "discovery" among his previous greats. He thus had the credentials to sell proposals for independent novels directly to hardcover book publishers, with serialization rights negotiated in addition to that. (Unlike real estate, a literary property can be sold to more than one buyer.)

The first of these independent novels was *Bill, the Galactic Hero* (1965). Written in Denmark at the risk of trusting his artistic impulse over his business sense, Harrison found its unusual mix of humor and science fiction hard to sell (as he feared; but he was not about to be typecast as the author of *Deathworld 23*). His initial contractor had backed out after reading it (fine adventure story, bad jokes). When it got around to Doubleday the science fiction editor there liked it, as did the one at the firm of Victor Golancz— Hilary Rubenstein who, later to join A. P. Watt & Son, the literary agency, became Harrison's lasting English agent. By the time this risk paid off, the Harrisons were back in London for a year, during which he also published *Plague from Space* (1966) and *Make Room! Make Room!* (1966). The latter title, although serialized in *Impulse* (August, September, October 1966), was originally contracted for in hard cover.

The Stainless Steel Rat Comes Out of His Hole

Before Harrison opened correspondence with John Campbell about *Deathworld 1*, he had already sold him a short story, "The Stainless Steel Rat," which appeared in ASF in August 1957. How this came about offers an interesting sidelight on the writer's imaginative life; anything at all can invade and occupy it. While struggling to develop his first novel, he idled through some old manuscript copy on which years earlier he had practiced writing "narrative hooks"—just the hooks without the stories that follow. A narrative hook, in the shoptalk of writers, is the brief copy on the bottom half of the first page of a manuscript under the title and byline, something that has to be lively and fascinating enough to "hook" the editor (and eventually the reader) into turning the page and going on with the rest of the story. Looking at one of these exercises, Harry got so hooked himself that he had to finish the story to find out what happened next. A related episode, "The Misplaced Battleship," appeared in *Analog* (April 1960) one month after the last installment of *Deathworld*. These two stories combined, with some fix-up and expansion, constitute *The Stainless Steel Rat* (1960). And so began the popular career of "Slippery" Jim diGriz in a whole series of "Rat" books, seven in all—eight, counting "An Interactive, Role-Playing Game," *You Can Be the Stainless Steel Rat* (1988).

The second and third Rat books, *The Stainless Steel Rat's Revenge* (1971) and *The Stainless Steel Rat Saves the World* (1971), were produced in rapid order after the Harrisons left London for a house in the quite distant suburbs of San Diego, California. One of Harrison's ambitions was to make contact with the Hollywood film industry, which he did to the extent that MGM produced a disappointing (to him) version of *Make Room! Make Room!*, released in 1973 as *Soylent Green*. I remember reading the horrible script before it was shot and hearing Harrison's woes at not being able to get a chance to revise a single line. But he made good use of his initial Hollywood explorations in *The Technicolor Time Machine* (1967), his comic masterpiece. It was also during these seven years in San Diego that he wrote what I regard as his literary masterpiece, *Captive Universe* (1968). In addition, there were three other novels, *In Our Hands, The Stars* (1969), *A Transatlantic Tunnel, Hurrah!*

(1972), *Star Smashers of the Galaxy Rangers* (1973); two juveniles, *Spaceship Medic* (1969) and *The Men from P.I.G. and R.O.B.O.T.* (1974) (with one more juvenile in 1975, *The California Iceberg*); and two short story collections, *Prime Number* (1969) and *One Step from Earth* (1970). He also published two crime novels, *Montezuma's Revenge* (1974) and *Queen Victoria's Revenge* (1974).

He also took time to teach an elective course on science fiction in Montgomery High School in San Diego, through the courtesy of Carol Pugner, chairman of the Journalism department, who was Todd's English teacher. This led to the joint development of a textbook anthology for high school use, *A Science Fiction Reader* (1973). At the same time he was teaching an extension course on science fiction at San Diego State University. As if all that were not enough, he was for two years (1976–78) publisher's first reader for Faber & Faber of London.

During the San Diego years, moreover, Harrison sustained a long editorial partnership with Brian Aldiss on several volumes of *Best SF* (1968–74), with two more volumes following as *The Year's Best SF* (1975–76). These were meant to be anthologies of purpose, the purpose being to make a critical statement as to what made for exemplary literature in this field. Harrison and Aldiss later collaborated to do three retrospective anthologies of like outlook for the best of three decades, the 1940s, the 1950s, and the 1960s. They also covered their idea of the best from ASF with *The Astounding-Analog Reader* in two volumes (1972–73).

What most impressed Harrison about Aldiss was that he combined excellence as a science fiction writer with astuteness as a book reviewer. After the two first met, they soon launched a project quite ahead of its time, "A Magazine of Criticism and Comment" called *SF Horizons*, which lasted only two issues (1964–65). But from this venture they learned to appreciate the shortcomings of the existing year's-best-science fiction type of anthology, such as annuals edited by Judith Merril, Donald Wolheim, Terry Carr, and Lester del Rey. Reaching higher critical standards, but inconsistently in their view, were the five volumes of the *Spectrum* series, edited by Kingsley Amis and Robert Conquest.

These latter volumes included introductions that sought to defend science fiction as a legitimate branch of literature against its hostile critics in the literary establishment, this when the tone of argument had every reason for being defensive, as it no longer need be (witness the science fiction authors appearing in Twayne's United States Authors Series). I asked Harrison about one point raised by Amis and Conquest, their justification of "flat" characters in science fiction, as against "round" ones in mainstream fiction (the typology is

E. M. Forster's from *Some Aspects of the Novel* [1927]). Amis and Conquest say, "characterization of the traditional sort would positively weaken and deflect most of the themes that typify [science fiction]."[13] To that idea, Harrison replied: "True for the short story, but not for the novel." He then cited *Greybeard* by Brian Aldiss: "A real novel and a real SF novel."

Some other anthologies of purpose are fitting for mention here, notably the *Nova* series, 1–4 (1970–74). A response to Damon Knight's *Orbit* series, these are what in the trade are called "hardback magazines," that is, their editors are not reprinters of stories from the magazines but solicitors of original stories for a series of hardcover books. To Harrison's way of thinking, however, Damon Knight was recruiting only one type of "artsy" story for *Orbit*, whereas *Nova* was to capture a range of artistry. The qualities that good science fiction shares with mainstream literature are highlighted in *The Light Fantastic: Science Fiction Classics from the Mainstream* (1971), which contains stories by Anthony Burgess, Mark Twain, Graham Greene, Jorge Luis Borges, Robert Graves, E. B. White, E. M. Forster, John Cheever, Rudyard Kipling, C. S. Lewis, and others.

Two other original anthologies of topical if not of critical interest are *The Year 2000* (1970) and *Astounding: John W. Campbell Memorial Anthology* (1973). This latter is a collection of original stories by ASF authors, all of whom had done serials or stories with sequels for Campbell. Here they tell the concluding episode, often with a humorous twist, to whatever old series they had contributed early on in their careers. Harry's own story, putting Jason dinAlt of the *Deathworld* trilogy into retirement, is "The Mothballed Spaceship." It is prefaced with his fond recollection of how the first of the series was developed with the editor's generous and knowing help:

I began writing *Deathworld* in 1956 in Mexico, continued it in England and Italy, and finally finished it in New York in 1957. All along it was a collaboration with John Campbell. Since I had already sold him a short story or two [the germs of the first Rat book], I felt bold enough to ask him to comment on an outline of a novel—my first—that I was struggling with. His answering letter was longer than my outline. He suggested ideas I had never considered, permutations never thought of—and all within the structure of my outline.[14]

Such was the manner in which Campbell cultivated his promising new authors. But going on from there, Harrison's own distinctive career has made him only the second after Robert Heinlein to make a full-time living through science fiction.

The Harrisons were settled for seven years near San Diego, until the city planned to drive a new highway right through the middle of their house. But Harrison was ready to pack up and leave in any case, back to Europe for good, because he felt a "dissatisfaction with life in a country that could commit the crimes of Vietnam and not be ashamed."[15] When I asked him if he regarded himself as an expatriate writer, he said, "No; I didn't *leave* the United States, I *went* to another country."

Settlement in Ireland

After spending 1974 in London, the Harrisons removed in 1975 to Ireland, the homeland of Harrison's grandmother on his father's side. As chance would have it I had some anthropological business in Ireland, sometime in the early 1980s and made sure of visiting the Harrisons in their new home, located on a mountainside and formerly owned by an architect who had designed it himself along modestly modern lines, overlooking the Vale of Avoca in County Wicklow. Just Harry and Joan lived there. Son Todd had remained in California where, following his father's interest in computers, he is working in R & D, building prototypes of newly invented medical machines. (He is the Todd Wells, the little boy of scientific curiosity of the juvenile, *The California Iceberg*.) Daughter Moira is now married to Eddie Guillot, a Dutchman she met while she was a student in Ireland, whose occupation is forestry management. Their home is Prospect Farm, in Cornwall, not far from Land's End, which is as far west as you can go in England before wading into the Atlantic Ocean.

Although Harry and Joan Harrison have now moved to a Dublin apartment, it was in County Wicklow that he completed his most innovative work to date, the *West of Eden* trilogy (1984–88). Before that, just to enumerate, his basement workshop there produced the *To the Stars* trilogy (1980–81), *Invasion Earth* (1980), *Planet of No Return* (1980), *Rebel in Time* (1983), and a revision of the 1972 Stonehenge novel we wrote together (1983). In a unique category is the illustrated novel, *Planet Story* (1979), done in an inspired collaboration with the English painter Jim Burns. I must also mention three other coffee-table picture books with nonfiction texts—*Great Balls of Fire: A History of Sex in Science Fiction Illustration* (1977), *Spacecraft in Fact & Fiction* (with the editor Malcolm Edwards, 1978), and *Mechanismo* (1978). Two non–science fiction titles are the technothriller, *Skyfall* (1976), and the terrorist thriller, *The QE2 Is Missing* (1980). Finally, there are the inevitable Rat books, all four of the remaining ones (not counting the game book), *The Stainless Steel Rat Wants You* (1978), *The Stainless Steel Rat for President* (1982), *A Stainless Steel Rat Is Born* (1985), and *The Stainless*

Steel Rat Gets Drafted (1987). These Rat books are immensely popular among Harrison's youngest fans, and they have even been turned into comic books, the "Rodent Series" for Eagle Comics in London.

The last title listed above has proved the most popular of all, helped along in the publicity and in book displays by the felicity of its cover art done by Jim Burns, an exacting painter of acrylics on hardboard as well as of oils on canvas. For his partial work in the science fiction field, he was (reluctantly) artist guest of honor at the 45th Worldcon, Brighton, England, in 1987, where he was introduced by Harry Harrison.[16] It was Harrison who had recognized his talent and who had lifted him up out of the comics and the doing of sensational paperback book covers, who in fact had to tear him away from all that and into the public eye with the thirty large oil paintings commissioned for *Planet Story*. "I had to *kick* Jim Burns into fame," Harrison says.

When I asked Harrison about books and sales, he delivered some useful information, starting with a little historical recital. Twenty years ago, he said, a good sale was twenty to thirty thousand copies. With reprints, the lifetime of any title may have extended another ten years, for the sale of maybe ten thousand more copies. In those days, book sales reached all the science fiction readers there were in the market; and they read everything. The writers had to wait for new fans to be born to get more sales. Now, today, first year sales are on a scale of from two hundred thousand to a quarter million copies; the market is up by a factor of ten. Last year (1987), science fiction amounted to 20 percent of the American book market—that's one science fiction and one fantasy novel per day—produced by six hundred members of Science Fiction Writers of America.

And where does Harry Harrison stand in this market? His answer: among the top twenty science fiction writers, only four of whom it can be said that all their novels have remained continuously in print. The others are Robert A. Heinlein, Arthur C. Clarke, and Isaac Asimov.

This led me on to ask about the working life of "The Science Fiction Professional," as Fred Pohl itemized the fourteen different jobs entailed. Harrison's responses (plus other matter I have thrown in) close out this biographical chapter. The listing, as it precedes Fred Pohl's own expansion on it, is taken from a symposium on writing titled, *The Craft of Science Fiction*. He says,

In order to be a real sf professional, you have to be able to function as:

1. A literary agent.
2. A contract lawyer.

3. A publicity man.
4. A performer—TV, radio, lectures.
5. An apparatnik, helping to keep professional and fan organizations functioning.
6. A teacher.
7. A critic.

And it helps if you are also skilled as:

8. A secretary.
9. An editor.
10. A proofreader.
11. A futurologist.
12. A scientist—at least to the extent of being able to understand and communicate what is happening in the marches of science.
13. An artist.

And, oh, yes—

14. A writer.[17]

Agent. Harrison says, "Any writer who is his own agent has a fool for a client." By that he means, the writer *alone* should not try to play the role of agent. His own way is to "sell" the publisher on a book, then the publisher goes to one of his agents, American or English, to settle the price. A special agent for movie rights is also called for, because Harrison is asked three or four times a year to sell or to renew film options on various book titles. Options run for one year, and they usually hold no more likelihood of leading to production than does a lottery ticket of winning. Still, Harrison is actively interested in this area, and he guesses that when he gets a winner, it will be for one of the Rat books. He has also written six commissioned screenplays (none of them produced; the same lottery effect operates even at this level), for which he is necessarily a member of the Screen Writer's Guild.[18]

Contract lawyer. A book contract is a legal document that basically specifies two sets of promises (what the publisher promises the author and vice versa) and indicates how the earnings are to be divided. On these matters, Harrison is an expert, and always assists his two literary agents in the writing of his contracts. With thirty-five books in print and a mass of old contracts on file, it pays to be alert at royalty payment time to spot defaults. Such a time came during my visit, when he found a sizeable chunk missing from one of his major American publishers (he knew from a glance at the royalty statement exactly what the amount should be). He then called his New York agent to take care of it.

P.R. Man. Every major publishing house has its promotion department, but the author himself has to take a hand in this business if it is to be effective. Harrison calls it "Promoting the promotion." That is why in his contracts he insists on getting big advances; otherwise the publisher has no self-interest in spending on a big advertising budget (the resulting sales recovering both the promotional costs and the advance). But Harry Harrison is by now so well established that publishers compete to have his name on their book lists. When my wife and I arrived in Cornwall, he had just returned from an author's tour of the United States, two months of TV talk shows, magazine and radio interviews, and public lectures on university campuses and elsewhere, all set up by Bantam Books, the publisher of his *West of Eden* trilogy. As a performer he entertains with the professional skill, as he says, of "a stand-up comedian."

Although some science fiction writers hire a special agent for booking lecture tours, Harrison does not. The only time he ever contracted with such an agency was when Crosby Productions, Inc. of La Jolla, California, came to him with a proposal to hit their lecture circuit on the subject of the film based on his novel about overpopulation, *Make Room! Make Room!*. The undated brochure promoting this (it had to be 1973 or shortly after) shows him in black tie (unprecedented!) and the title is, "*Soylent Green*: An Image of Tomorrow?"

Another aspect of P.R. is book signing, at a major outlet at time of publication, at specialty science fiction bookstores, and at the various science fiction conventions. At Windycon 13, here in Chicago in 1987, he signed five thousand copies of various titles (most of them Rat books, it seemed). One fan hauled in a whole cartonful of books—the complete works of Harry Harrison—to be signed.

Apparatnik. Harrison's life in organized fandom began very early, in 1938, with membership in the Queens chapter of the Science Fiction League. The fannish word "fiawol," an acronym for "fandom is a way of life," indicates that science fiction fandom is not a normal hobby group. Harrison the science fiction pro is just a grown-up fan, who enjoys the conventions as much as he appreciates the P.R. benefits from being invited to them as guest of honor, where the science fiction writer has the opportunity, unique to his genre, of addressing a captive readership. These things can get very big, especially the worldcons, which have in the past exceeded eight thousand attendance.

It helps, in getting invitations, to assist with the programming at other times and to answer one's fan mail. At regional conventions, from 1962, Harrison has been guest of honor more than a dozen times, in England, the U.S., Australia, Japan, Scotland, Ireland, even Denmark. But no matter how far he travelled, the convention managers paid his air fare, plus local transport, the hotel, food, and bar bill, and what is called "walking about money" ($100.00 a day).

As for the professional organizations for science fiction writers, he was chairman of the first such, as already noted, in New York City in 1950; and he was active in forming Science Fiction Writers of America (1965), for which he designed the SFWA logo. Since then he has gone on to help found World SF, with himself "reluctantly" elected as its first president.

This grew out of the first International Science Fiction Writers Conference that he organized in Dublin in 1976, with the backing of the Arts Council and other agencies of the Irish government. The result was a good international showing, with as many editors and publishers as there were writers in attendance, about one hundred in all, and the happy signing of contracts on all sides. The advantage of Ireland as a locale in drawing foreign authors from Eastern Europe was its neutrality as a country not part of NATO. Harrison paid a visit to the Soviet embassy in Dublin to discuss the attendance of certain Russian science fiction writers he knew, since the U.S.S.R. and Ireland had no agreement on cultural relations. What he got was a delegation of Hungarian and Bulgarian writers testing the waters for the Russians who, sure enough, showed up for the second Dublin conference in 1978, together with the chairman of the science fiction branch of the Writers Union—and the chairman of the Soviet Writers Union himself.

At this point it should be mentioned that Harrison is the one most popular American science fiction writer to be read in translation, and, indeed, one of the most popular of all American authors both in Russian and a number of the minority languages of the U.S.S.R. That fact, somehow impacting the Moscow literary scene, surely worked to his advantage in persuading the Writers Union of the U.S.S.R. to sponsor the next go-around; the Third International Science Fiction Writers Conference was held there in 1987, a cultural event of novel openness for Soviet Russia.[19] But as Harrison says, "SF is the largest international literary movement in the world."

At these affairs, World SF gives out the Karel Award for best translator (named after Karel Čapek), and the President's Award for "independence of thought in the field of SF." What Harrison did not tell me about (I learned of it from a newsletter mailed out by the World SF U.S. National Secretary) is the Harry Harrison Award, "for improving the status of SF internationally."[20]

Teacher.   Harrison's first response to this point was to recall that he had taught Esperanto while in art school. But I will defer an account of his elevated place in the Esperanto movement until chapter 9, which deals with the Rat books (one of them carries at the back advice on how to contact the movement).

Harrison happily accepts invitations to lecture on university and college campuses, here and abroad, but he is just as able to stand up before the professorate at its own academic meetings. During his U.S. book tour in the summer of 1988, for example, he made a stop at the Nineteenth Annual Conference of the Science Fiction Research Association to lecture, at a special session given him, on "Science Fiction and the Death of God."[21] Perhaps here is a good place to mention his important lecture at the Institute of Contemporary Arts in London, on "Worlds beside worlds" (the parallel worlds theme in Science Fiction).[22]

But his main response to the item at hand was to stress the "didactism of the genre." That is to say, science fiction is quite a content-oriented literature, with message-as-content. Later he went on to explain the special problems of writing in this genre.

Critic. Here he recalled *SF Horizons*, the first magazine of professional science fiction criticism, which aborted after two issues because it was too far ahead of its time. The problem he was reacting to with this effort was the lack of comparative vision among both academic critics and fannish critics: "They all took each writer as if he stood alone, each story as if it had no parallels." The year's best anthologies with Brian Aldiss were also a critical exercise, in that they aimed to teach by example what good science fiction is.

Secretary. "Well, I know how to type." Harrison means that he is facile with his word processor and office computer, which keeps all his letter files and manuscript copy in orderly and accessible storage.

Editor. First and foremost is the importance of self-editing. Harrison, quoting Hemingway, says: "Every successful writer must have an in-born shit detector." A good writer also respects good editing from a competent copyeditor.

Proofreader. "Proof it yourself," is Harrison's motto. He and his computer alone do all the proofreading.

Futurologist. Harrison follows John Campbell's dictum on this. Because science fiction can be about the past, the present, or the future, futurology is called into play only for *some* science fiction.

Scientist. "Every SF writer should be a fan of science." That many are not is why so much bad science fiction is written. "The bad SF writer is lazy," he says elsewhere, addressing fellow SFWA members. "Why do the research to write a parallel world novel when a fantasy novel can be ground out without opening another book? Science is one of the two words in science fiction, but the bad writer doesn't care. Too lazy again to keep track of the technology, the science, the theories that change our world hourly. Easier to write another boring fantasy novel."[23]

Artist. In the literary sense, Harrison explains, the art of science fiction is not unlike the art of writing mystery stories. In both cases, "the story is back plotted. You know what you want to do and where to go." Take, for example, *The Time Machine* by H. G. Wells. He knew the ending, and worked back from there. "The back-plotting is the construction, the *craft* of science fiction; but disguising it is the *art* of science fiction."

Science fiction differs from mainstream fiction, in which the principal art is building character; for mainstream fiction, "the characters *are* the plot, whereas in SF characters are made to fit the plot." And while this method may result in characters more "flat" than "round" ("but not so 'flat' that if they turn sideways they vanish!"), it should never become an excuse for bad writing. The story, artistically done, must be both well told and well written. Of course it is possible to have a story that is well told and not well written—an apt example is Theodore Dreiser's *Sister Carrie* of which Harrison says "You have to fight the prose to find the story." Thus the distinction between telling and writing is one to bear in mind, the better to cultivate both with conscious artistry.

That Harry Harrison practices what he preaches is no better illustrated than by the one line below from a sensitive review of *Winter in Eden*, the second volume of his *West of Eden* trilogy: "Harrison's prose is, as always, a literate delight, and his story-telling gifts have never been stronger."[24]

Writing. "Writing is the imparting of information." In nonfiction, like essay writing, this is imparted directly in so many words. But in fiction the rule is, "Don't tell 'em, show 'em!" (To tell in this case means explanation and does *not* have the same meaning as in "storytelling.") New information that is part of the story must be brought into it by way of dialogue and action; abstract information must be converted into physical fact that can be demonstrated. Harrison then gives "One Step from Earth" as an example, the first story from a collection of that title, a story drawing for its background upon scientific data about the atmosphere of Mars. From the Viking Program lander (Mariner 4, 1965), he learned that while Mars's atmospheric pressure is like Earth's, it has no water vapor. To show and not tell this information, Harrison introduced a mouse onto the surface of Mars: "All abstract knowledge about Martian atmospherics is acted out in the fate of that mouse."

Two other rules. "One, never use a long word when a short one will do, as 'dry' for 'dessicate.' Two, don't waffle on technical terms. If there's no other word for it, don't work around it. Define it in context, as does C. S. Forester his nautical terms in the sea stories." The artistic aim here is to work for "efficient prose." Related to that aim is the goal of "precision," with everything in the story put there for a reason. A single-idea story, containing one extra word is "overwritten."

Message content (another kind of information), too, should be concealed within the entertaining story line itself. "If the message is obvious, it's a bad book." In some cases entertainment is more important than message, as with the Rat books. The reverse occurs with *Make Room! Make Room!*. But even here, where the message is the author's main concern, his reader is carried along by the gripping story for one-third of the novel before he comes to one character asking another, "Why is the world so bad?" The following lecture of 230 words, covering about two or three pages, is something unusual in a Harrison book. But, as he says, "One little bit of pointed rhetoric goes a long way." Usually Harrison conceals his messages and entertainment comes first.

On impulse I asked him a crazy question. "Why entertainment? Why fiction?" Only Harry Harrison would try to really answer that. "Language is the most distinctive thing about Man as a primate, then came writing, the greatest invention since the discovery of fire, and so now books are the most important thing in the world to us. Entertainment in writing is the crowning achievement of the human primate. Think of it! Information processed as entertainment by readers willing to suspend disbelief for stories told as lies. The highest input function of the brain is reading fiction."

Chapter Three
Citizen of the Universe

The role of science in the science fiction of Harry Harrison is what it was for Robert Boyle, a charter member of the Royal Society and the author of *The Sceptical Chemist* (1661)—a good in and of itself that frees man's mind from dogma and superstition. Boyle's experiments, the first to be so described that anybody might repeat and thus confirm them, had the philosophical purpose of liberating opinion from the control then exercised by a politically established church. The honest methods and true results of his chemistry challenged faith in an age of absolutism; that was his contribution as a secular intellectual of the sort who formed the Royal Society, and whose motto was *Nullis in Verba* (Nothing by mere authority). The chemist must be a skeptic first and foremost, before he can be useful in a practical way. Boyle is the great scientific hero of the Enlightenment, that philosophical movement of the seventeenth and eighteenth centuries characterized by a belief in the power of reason, and by innovations in political, economic, and religious doctrine.

From this movement grew the socialism of Saint-Simon, a new political religion, and eventually the science fiction of Jules Verne and H. G. Wells. Their preoccupation with the peaceful production of wealth, and methods of equitable distribution, stems from the Enlightenment view that extremes of wealth and poverty are not only morally wrong but a hindrance to economic growth. This idea is obvious enough today, but centuries ago it challenged the dominant theological view that poverty was ordained by God. To the enlightened, however, poverty was the source of ignorance, crime, disease, and widespread misery, not to say the foundation for tyrannical government and its unchecked disposition to wage war. All of these evils the enlightened traced to their essential cause in what they called "superstition." Perhaps in rejecting the church they also discarded the wisdom of Christianity in its basic teaching that evil is latent in the hearts of men, a fixed constant not subject to erasure by any political, economic, social, or religious means. At all events, this new faith in reason, as a guide to universal welfare and happiness, was given to the promotion of wealth, knowledge, and freedom—freedom from dogma and tyranny—as a set of interconnected values. The enlightened thus proclaimed their belief in what present-day liberals describe as human rights.[1]

We can trace a line of descent from the preliberals of the Enlightenment, through the nineteenth-century *laissez-aller* liberals who favored limited government as a means of safekeeping individual rights, to the collectivist liberals of today who defend welfare legislation as a means of upholding social rights. A strong state, once thought bad, is now thought to be good when it serves human rights defined in the collective.

Although Harrison identifies himself as a liberal writer, it is not all that easy to place him in the above scheme, given that his books are full of contradictions that derive from his knowingly cutting across the different ideological eras just outlined. As he says, "I am very conscious writer." I hope my readers will not think that I am overstating the intellectual content of Harrison's works, even though they seem to be filled with inconsistencies from the standpoint of the typical twentieth-century literary liberal.

The works treated in this chapter, whatever else they may be, are especially notable for their conscious closeness to preliberal thought. Nowhere is this more evident than in his finest and most artful short story, "Rescue Operation." One need not agree with the case it argues—for it is an argument as well as a moving story—to appreciate its craft. It demonstrates the literary merit that Harrison at his best strives to bring to science fiction, even as it states his rationalist faith in the saving grace of science to rescue mankind from its premodern follies. This story alone might well stand as a compact summary of the Enlightenment ideal. For its controlled unity of form and content, it deserves recognition as a masterly example of the American short story.

"Rescue Operation"

"Rescue Operation," the author notes, "is a real story, happening in a real place. The characters, with one exception, are real, and I have met them all. I have walked this particular island and bathed in this sea. While doing so the idea for this story presented itself fullblown."

The author here refers to an island in the Adriatic, just off the coast of Yugoslavia. He continues his background briefing as follows: "Yugoslavia is probably the most primitive country in Europe. Wild, barren, fought over for centuries, populated by differing groups and nations, it has been a-bubble with factionalism since the memory of man. When the Germans invaded it during the Second World War the partisan bands took to the hills with their guns. And fought with each other first before turning on the

Nazis." Of course, he goes on to note, things have changed under the rule of
Marshall Tito with parts of the country finally brought into the twentieth
century—but not the part visited by Harrison on a camping holiday with his
family. He continues:

> I was one of the first postwar travellers to penetrate some of these distant places and I
> had a good view of life as it has been lived there for centuries. Not the most entranc-
> ing as you can well imagine. Yet there is a Yugoslavian nuclear institute.
>   Yugoslavia is a microcosm that reflects our entire world. In that hot sunlight I saw,
> suddenly, how by the addition of a familiar science fiction device I could make it
> stand for the whole.[2]

That device, a visitor from some remote part of the cosmos, is what gives
the story its global significance. Hence the title of this chapter, which is a
phrase from Voltaire, the most eminent of the Enlightenment thinkers. The
phrase appears (with my italics) in the following passage from his *Philosophical Dictionary* (1764), under the heading of *Patrie* (Fatherland):

> It is sad that, to be a good patriot, one is often the enemy of the rest of humanity. . . .
> To be a good patriot is to want one's city to be enriched by commerce and powerful in
> arms. It is obvious that a country cannot gain unless another loses, and that it cannot
> vanquish without causing unhappiness.
>   So it is the human condition that to wish for the greatness of one's fatherland is to
> wish evil to one's neighbors. The *citizen of the universe* would be the man who wishes
> his country never to be either greater or smaller, richer or poorer.[3]

To make a science fiction story of this idea, it is necessary to view its characters as having importance not as individuals but only in relationship to humanity at large. Opposed to this method is the literary theory, well expressed
by D. H. Lawrence, that in the art of fiction, "individual lives cannot be ag-
gregated or equated or dealt with quantitatively in any way."[4] Thus it is a
prejudice of the literary critics that such a story, however excellent as a work of
genre literature, must remain outside the canon of true literature, where intellectual content—idea as hero—has no place by definition.

But the characters in "Rescue Operation" are no less interesting for their
lack of selfhood transformed by experience or some other aspect of individual
fullness. They are real enough for the author's purpose. Moreover, the measured precision of the prose in achieving the story's overall effect of unearthly
sanity is as much an object of attention as the narrative subject.

The story, told by an omniscient narrator, opens with two fishermen,

Dragomir and Pribislav Polasek, out in the Gulf of Kvarneric casting their net. Not wholly reduced to rustic stereotypes, they are given just enough personality to differentiate between the more dominant Dragomir (tagged only by his last name) and the lesser Pribislav (first name tag, a subtle touch). Their different parts, in discussing what they have caught in their net, inform the reader of the situation in a more revealing and interesting way than would direct exposition.

What they have caught is a man (in a space suit, as it turns out), who seems to have waved his hand as he fell out of the net. Is he alive? It is hard to say in the dark, with only the light from the lamp in the bow of the boat. The fishermen discuss their problem and decide they need help. Dragomir urges that they go for the "diver, the one who stays with the widow Korenc, he will know what to do. His name is Kukovic and Petar said he is a doctor of science from the university in Ljubjana." This is Dr. Joze Kukovic, a nuclear physicist and the story's figure of sanity and reason, now on a scuba-diving vacation at the island town of Brbinj. (A local geography, if it is to be universalized, must in the first instance be specified, as with the place names and other linguistic usages that the author introduces to that end.)

Dr. Kukovic comes on the scene early the next morning while having coffee on the porch of his guest house and looking down the unpaved and dusty street leading to the port, already astir with its primitive market, donkeys, and women as beasts of burden. The sun has just come up, but "It was hot already. Brbinj was a town at the edge of nowhere, locked between the empty ocean and barren hills, asleep for centuries and dying by degrees. There were no attractions here—if you did not count the sea." The day before "he had found a Roman galley half-buried in the sand. He would get into it today, the first human in two thousand years." The distance separating ancient Rome from "modern" Brbinj, a town that has changed little over the centuries, is as nothing compared to the distance separating modern Brbinj from the civilization of the alien.

The fisherman break in on Kukovic. Dragomir scarcely knows how to begin, but pointing out over the ocean he says,

"It fell out there last night, we saw it, a *sputnik* without a doubt."

"A traveller?" Joze Kukovic wrinkled his forehead not quite sure he heard right. When the locals were excited it was hard to follow their dialect. For such a small country Yugoslavia was cursed with a multitude of tongues.

"No, it was not a *putnik*, but a *sputnik*, one of the Russian spaceships."

"Or an American one," Pribislav spoke for the first time, but he was ignored.

Joze smiled and sipped his coffee. "Are you sure it wasn't a meteorite you saw?

There is always a heavy meteor shower at this time of year."

"A *sputnik*," Dragomir insisted stolidly. "The ship fell far out in the *Jadransko More* and vanished, we saw that. But the space pilot came down almost on top of us, into the water. . . . "

Dr. Kukovic is now astonished into alertness and action as he learns the essential details: the pilot caught in the net, then lost—"he was in a heavy suit, with a window like a diving suit, and there was something on his back that might have been like your tanks there."

Kukovic determines to find the pilot. The place is marked with a buoy, but a physician may be needed. "You have none here, but is there one in Osor?" "Dr. Gratos, but he is very old." Well, he will have to do, but neither of the two fishermen know how to drive Joze's car so as to go fetch him. But Dragomir remembers that Petar had been a partisan, and had driven stolen German trucks. Kukovic hands his car keys to Dragomir to give to Petar, who is to bring the doctor at once. Dragomir hands them to Pribislav because he himself intends to go with Kukovic, on the more important rescue mission in the Gulf.

After they row out to the buoy, offshore from Trstenic, Joze dives down to the bottom and finds the man in his pressure suit. It has no markings on it, American or Russian, and is made of unearthly material, hard as steel yet flexible. The man inside, seen through the face plate, alive and with eyes open, is not human. Kukovic's fear of the unknown is overpowered by his curiosity and his sympathy when he sees that the creature's right leg is crushed. He carries the alien to the surface. The stolid Dragomir is all fear when he sees what the physicist has brought up from below. "You great stupid clumsy clod of a peasant, help me," shouts Kukovic, struggling to get the alien on board, but Dragomir only retreats to the far end of the boat. Now it is Joze's turn to be alarmed, as he notes the helmet filled with water—the creature is drowning! But wait; better *not* try to open the suit: "Had the water leaked in—or was it possible it had always been there? Who knew what alien atmosphere it might breathe; methane, chlorine, sulphur dioxide—why not water? The liquid was inside, surely enough, the suit wasn't leaking and the creature seemed unchanged." Reason prevails, even in the midst of a panic to do the right thing that might be the wrong thing.

Rowing the boat back to the harbor with terrified strokes, Dragomir leaps ashore, kicking the boat adrift in his fright. Kukovic throws a mooring line out; nobody from among the crowd of backward shuffling peasants, blank-faced, crossing themselves, will pick it up. The bad tidings have spread, the whole mob now sharing "the same fear of the unknown." Only a feeble-minded youth at last answers Kukovic's cries and pulls on the rope.

Bearing the alien in his arms, Joze is headed for his room, the only safe place he thinks, when a newcomer pushes through the crowd of hostile watchers to confront him. It is Father Perc:

"There—what is that? A *vrag*." The old priest pointed in horror at the alien in Joze's arms and backed away, fumbling for his crucifix.
"Enough of your superstition!" Joze snapped. "This is no devil but a sentient creature, a traveller. . . . It is a creature from another world, a water-breathing animal, and it's hurt. We must help it."

But the priest is unmoved. " 'It is wrong,' he mumbled, 'this is something unclean, *zao duh*. . . . ' "

Back home with the alien on his bed, Joze hears his car returning, but no one appears—the townspeople are briefing Dr. Bratos. Then he and Petar enter. With the help of Petar (the more cosmopolitan for having been a partisan, even though he thinks the thing before him quite ugly), Kukovic tests the liquid from the suit—warm salt water, about 120 degrees, with a trace of iodine—and then fills the bathtub with same, placing the alien in it after removing the suit. The creature's leg is bleeding, and Kukovic urges the reluctant Dr. Bratos to apply a pressure bandage (it is only a traumatic injury), warning him not to use any drugs or antiseptics that might kill the creature with its alien body chemistry.

The alien then reaches into a container attached to the discarded suit and pulls out some object, handing it to Joze. It is a book of some kind—what a priceless treasure of advanced knowledge it must hold! But his dreams are cut short by the convulsive death spasms of the alien, killed, as the doctor had secretly hoped, by the application of sulfanilamide.

While agonizing over the alien's death, Kukovic notes the entrance of Father Perc, who picks up the book, rushes into the kitchen and throws it on the fire of the woodstove, where it burns up almost instantly, being made of some highly inflammable material:

" 'It was evil,' said the priest from the doorway. 'A *zao duh*, an abomination with a book of evil. We have been warned, such things have happened before on earth, and always the faithful must fight back—' " Now, with a fit of Byronic world-weariness, Joze falls to a chair where he mourns aloud:

"Why here?" he asked. "Of all places in the world why here? A few more degrees to the west and the creature would have come down near Trieste with surgeons, hospitals, men, facilities. Or, if it had just stayed on course a little longer, it could have seen lights, and would have landed at Rijika [formerly Fiume]. Something could have been done. But why here?" He surged to his feet, shaking his fist at nothing—and at everything.

"Here, in this superstition-ridden, simple-minded backwater of the world! What kind of world do we live in where there is a five million volt electron accelerator not a hundred miles from primitive stupidity. That this creature should come so far, come so close . . . why, why?"

The answer to that question is given in the double meaning of the story's title. The rescue operation ͺ save the alien failed not only because of local superstition in this backwater place, but also because "primitive stupidity" in the rest of the world—the dogmas of selfish patriotism among its great nations—allows such unhappy places to exist. (Voltaire would endorse this idea.) And so fails the rescue of planet Earth from the injustice of its Third World enclaves; for in the alien's book of superenlightenment, as Joze dreamed, was a knowledge of advanced science and technology that would have lifted mankind with ease to such a high level of universal development and prosperity that war, commercial or military, would have no justification. With that superior knowledge coming to men from some cosmic source, they could have united in a collective effort for development and the conquest of nature, want, and misery.

Thus does the author portray Yugoslavia as a part (with its electron accelerator and its Brbinj) standing for the whole (the world with its modern and underdeveloped countries.) If underdevelopment exists in the so-called Third World, it does so at a cost to all humanity; backward Brbinj has global consequences. In holding such a view, Harrison remains a preliberal child of the Enlightenment, remote from the liberal position that may be tagged as bleeding heart Third-Worldism. This latter stance is typified by F. R. Leavis, who indicts "the energy, the triumphant technology, the productivity [and] the high standard of living" that belongs to the modern world for its "life-impoverishment," and who compares it with "a Bushman, an Indian peasant, or a member of those poignantly surviving peoples, with their marvelous art and skills and vital intelligence." It is also the stance of technophobic science fiction. "Machines that master men," for example, is the pitch made for a theme anthology edited by Damon Knight.[5] But for Harry Harrison, who is not shy to speak for "machine as hero," there is nothing poignant about underdevelopment; its backwardness equals primitive stupidity.

Planet of the Damned

All of this is plain enough in "Rescue Operation," a story whose realism sets out to familiarize the reader with the unlovely facts of the case. But elsewhere he uses the technique of defamiliarization, or what Ezra Pound called "making strange,"[6] to make the same point, as in *Planet of the Damned* and its sequel, *Planet of No Return*. Here, a fantastic whole stands for a realistic part. A galaxy of different, single-landscape planets, even as Earth is one such in these novels of the far future, is given to represent actual multiformity; and our familiar problems are brought home by making them look newly discovered and strangely distant. The novels' hero, an agent of CRF (the Cultural Relationships Foundation) and a true citizen of the universe, goes about rescuing whole worlds from superstition. The blurb on the back of the first novel in the series states his mission:

Brion Brandd of the Galactic CRF had a problem. It was the planet Dis. Brion's assignment was to salvage it.

Dis was a harsh, inhospitable, dangerous place and the Disans made it worse. They might have been human once—but they were something else now.

The Disans had only one desire—kill! Kill everything, themselves, their planet, the universe if they could.

Brion had minutes to stop them—if he could find out how![7]

In this mission, Brion works in collaboration with a biologist, Lea Morees, because an ecological puzzle must be solved before anything practical can be done. He and she form a research team on the model of scientific collegiality as practiced in the laboratories of modern industry. Their job is to research a problem and apply the solution to a new product—in this case, a peaceful culture. In short, their business is cultural engineering, or social R & D. The CRF is a world-saving moral enterprise, whose agents carry out its assignments in programmed innovation with the R & D methods of industrial enterprise.

Mission-oriented R & D, of course, was introduced to modern science fiction by Hugo Gernsback with the title hero of *Ralph 124C41+*, modeled after Arthur D. Little. But it was John W. Campbell who more closely reflected the commonplace aspect of the research revolution with its emphasis on laboratory teamwork. The heroes of his "Arcot, Morey and Wade" series are attached to the research department of a multinational (no, multiplanetary!) corporation, for whom they as a team take on problems in the field of pure observational science with a view to finding profitable application in their solutions. Another story group, the "Penton and Blake" series, does not have its heroes commercially linked to industry. The heroes are a pair of cosmic explorers who land on various planets and there enjoy collegiality in the solving of exotic scientific puzzles for mere intellectual pleasure. Here Campbell isolates the research side of the R & D equation to show that the power to determine the material world by means of industrial science must rest, in the first instance, upon the power to observe that world.[8]

The mission of CRF is to determine the cultural world in like manner. Brion and Lea undergo their collegial heroics in the cause of instituting peace and plenty. Harrison science-fictionalizes a formula of Bertrand Russell's which, in "Artificially Created Societies," states that "no society can be regarded as fully scientific unless it has been created deliberately with a certain structure to fulfill certain purposes."[9] Harrison's faith in that formula derives from his "humanistic morality," whose moral output is delivered by the CRF by means of a science called "Societics." This applied science is first mooted in a pilot story for the two novels in question, so it is best to turn aside, for the moment, to briefly consider it.

The story is titled, "The K-Factor,"[10] where the CRF is revealed to be an agency of "the UN," now become a world government, or better, the government of a galactic federation or empire centered on a planet not Earth, following its colonization somewhere in the most distant reaches of the sidereal universe. The CRF takes a cosmic view of man and society as "a system problem that can be fed into a computer." And Societics is the science making that possible. It is defined as "The applied study of the interaction of individuals in a culture, the interaction of the group generated by these individuals, the equations derived therefrom, and the application of these equations to control one or more factors of this same culture." In short, it is a kind of social physics. The one factor the CRF is ever alert to control is the k-factor—"k" for killing, it seems, because "The k-factor is the war factor." Says the head of CRF, "Our planetary operators have two jobs. First to gather and interpret data. Secondly to keep the k-factor negative." Thus, "a good survey is half the problem" in the social R & D equation that, when a "violence-oriented society" is detected, can be applied to prevent the k-factor from going positive, that is, by eliminating those "individuals and groups who [are] k-factor amplifiers."

But for all of the R & D chatter with which Societics is mystified, its research half reduces to espionage and its applied half to the assassination of key individuals or the repression of troublesome groups. Behind Societics is a political authority whose directive is: find the war lovers, the "jingoists with low I.Q.'s," and get rid of them. So much for moral entrepreneurship!

Yet Harrison tells me that there are no villains in his books; he does not believe in villains, nor in "the superstitious, Catholic devil theory of evil. There is a *reason* for evil." In this case, the reason seems to be the existence of unreasonable men who do not believe in the Brotherhood of Man. Thus, because they fall outside the brotherhood of the doctrine, as it were, they are fair game for punishment by an arm of government given to coercive ethical and social improvement.

The story's CRF assassin is, however, a bit saddened by this necessary murder. His meditation on the matter echoes that of Bertrand Russell in facing up to the same idea, when he said of the scientific outlook that it might well serve to mask something else: "The pleasure of planned construction is one of the most powerful motives in men who combine intelligence with energy; whatever can be constructed according to plan, such men will endeavor to construct . . . the desire to create is not in itself idealistic since it is a form of the love of power, and while the power to create exists there will be men desirous of using this power even if unaided nature would produce a better result than any that can be brought about by deliberate intention."[11]

Likewise, the hero of "The K-Factor" reflects on the nature of his power to do the planetary good he has just done, in keeping its k-factor down to a peaceful level: "Power, perhaps that's the keyword. . . . We have the stars now but we have carried with us our little personal lusts and emotions."

Here is dramatized the schizoid condition of modern liberalism in its dual aspects of power and freedom. While men have freed themselves to become "citizens of the universe," in Voltaire's phrase, they still are prompted by the *libido dominandi* or power motive to make for unhappiness in the coercive sway of political authority. The liberal's traditional concern with liberty is expressed in the story as a reaching to the stars although what is today heralded as liberation is not freedom from too much government, but a sky's-the-limit, anything goes freedom in the arts and in personal morality. But liberalism also consecrates the state to social reconstruction in expanding choices available to the "victims of society," the poor and the marginal. This is expressed in the story by the power motive that CRF's agent agonizes over. The agony of liberalism is real enough: if political liberty of the individual must be restricted or even sacrificed to enforce the liberal's ideal of social justice, then its twin or paired ideal, that of individualism in morality, art, and literature, begins to look uncomfortably like a cultural bribe offered in exchange for passive acceptance of statist controls over the economy. This is the very same compensatory hedonism satirized in Aldous Huxley's antiliberal novel, *Brave New World* (1932). Robert Nisbet, author of another *Philosophical*

Dictionary after Voltaire's, phrases this dilemma as the tension between "the liberalism of statism and of cultural license."[12]

At all events, with the spirit of energy and intelligence cautiously admired by Bertrand Russell, Brion Brandd and Lea Morees look ahead to their next assignment for CRF. Says Brion, "Aren't [we] going to have a fine time designing a social structure that is a little more responsible to the people than the present one" (*Planet of No Return*, chapter 10). They certainly had a fine time of it on their other two cases.

Brion is first recruited to the Cultural Relationships Foundation in *Planet of the Damned*. The title planet is Dis, a desert-like world where the ecological adaptations of its life-forms, plants, animals and humans, is a puzzle to be solved before the k-factor in its political leadership can be understood and controlled. Brion himself comes from a single-culture planet, where peaceful competition has been realized in a set of annual games, called the Twenties, which range from chess to fencing. The top contenders face a tough ordeal, as they contend for months with the wits and strength of everybody who enters the games, a wide-open kind of participatory Olympics. Noncompetitors follow the games with a sense of planetary patriotism. Universal faith in the Twenties is what makes of every citizen a "scientific humanist," the entire population rejoicing in its peaceful unanimity.

As a new winner, elevated to global glory, Brion is approached by CRF for his polymathic skills. He shows no interest, and does not seem to care about the significance of his world's progressive achievement as a peaceful planet "in a galaxy filled with warring, hate-filled, backward planets." So his recruiter sends him on a guilt trip:

"All of you haven't a single thought for the past, for the untold billions who led the bad life as mankind slowly built up the good life for you to lead. Do you ever think of all the people who suffered in misery and superstition while civilization was clicking forward one more notch?"

"Of course I don't think about them," Brion retorted. "Why should I? I can't change the past."

"But you can change the future!" [says the recruiter]. "You owe something to the suffering ancestors who got you where you are today. If Scientific Humanism means anything more than just words to you, you must possess a sense of responsibility. Don't you want to try and pay off a bit of this debt by helping others who are just as backward and disease-ridden today as great-grandfather Troglodyte ever was?" (*Planet of the Damned*, chapter 2)

After Brion is won over, he is introduced to Societics (together with the revelation that his own planet is a product of CRF planning): "As with all of the other sciences, we have found out that the more we know, the more there is to know. We no longer attempt to guide cultures towards what we consider a beneficial goal. There are too many goals, and from our limited vantage point it is hard to tell the good ones from the bad ones" (chapter 3). So far, this is good Enlightenment doctrine. While its philosophers believed that reason would lead to happiness, they could not define this good; they agreed only in the causes of evil. And the CRF certainly knows what evils it wants to eliminate from its hopeful prospects. In hopeless cases, however, planets where the progressive spirit of change is not alive at all—well, the policy then is to "bury the dead ones." As for happiness in its multiplex goals, if men were left to their own devices they would only quarrel over the choice, so the CRF decides what will make for a happy society—freedom from indisputable social ills—and then enforces the decision. Its means are those of statist liberalism carried to despotic lengths, for "The technique [is] to work out an artificial culture that would be most beneficial for a planet, then bend it into the mold." The CRF treats people as objects of welfare, a sort of liberation-fodder not unlike Napoleon's cannon-fodder.

With that background briefing on "humanistic morals," Brion is dispatched to Dis with the biologist Lea. The problem there is that its ruling class, the magters, not only oppress their own people, but also possess atomic missiles aimed at a neighboring planet, the Scandinavian-like Nyjord. In unriddling the Disian ecology, which seems to be a troublesome factor, Brion and Lea uncover a curious and all-pervading system of symbiosis. Brion finds a symbiote living in the brain of a dead magter, whose body he secures for Lea's dissection in a shoot-'em-up commando raid on one of the magter strongholds. So that's it! A symbiote—no, a true parasite in this case—has displaced the magter frontal lobes from childhood. With their centers of reason eaten away, no wonder the magters are all killer maniacs. No devil is called for; "They are *forced* to be evil," as Harrison explained to me. All the same, they will have to be destroyed so as to allow a new generation to grow up free of the affliction. The magters are eliminated, and the missile base is taken out at the last minute before firing. The mission ends with Brion and Lea receiving gratitude and much pay (it is possible to do well by doing good) from Nyjord, the target planet. Too pacifist to defend itself, Nyjord had, in the pinch, supplied a secret commando army. Its pacifism itself is a CRF product, but a CRF officer was able to prevail upon its president, by way of collecting an I.O.U. for his installation, to give the needed help.

Planet of No Return

Next mission. On the back cover of the novel relating it, the blurb says, "Now, in this stunning illustrated sequel, [Brion Brandd's] going to learn that even when it comes to world-saving some jobs are easier than others— because the *Planet of the Damned* was a piece of candy compared to what's waiting for him on *Planet of No Return*." The book is indeed richly illustrated, an expensive sign of its publisher's faith in massive sales—which proved to be true.

On Selm-II, the CRF detects a vast battlefield of ruined war machines, and loses two agents looking into the matter. Time to send in Brion; and although no biologist is really called for on this case, Lea tags along for the love interest and for the purpose of making dialogue, but in the event proves useful.

They land far from the battlefield, and soon run into a camp of real troglo-dytes, cave dwellers who are so primitive and miserable, not to say childish in their prelogical, taboo-ridden behavior and limited vocabulary, that they have no fire and eat their meat (giant reptiles) raw. This reflects the Enlight-enment view of primitive man in the childhood of the race, the starting point of progress, a view derived from the medieval legend of the wild man (*homme sauvaige*). From this outlook, even contemporary "natives" were seen to be relics of their prehistoric ancestors, as in the now outdated anthropology of Lucien Lévi-Bruhl presented in his *Primitive Mentality* (1923) and *How Na-tives Think* (1926). Stories about prehistoric cavemen of little culture entered popular fiction from 1887 with "Christmas 200,000 B.C." by Stanley Water-loo, collected in *The Wolf's Howl* (1899).[13] It is well known to science fiction writers working this field, as are two stories by H. G. Wells, "A Story of the Stone Age" (1897) and "The Grisly Folk" (1921). Caveman primitivity in proto–science fiction, often associated with prehistoric monsters, continued its popularity in Vincent Hamlin's comic strip of the 1930s about Alley Oop, the caveman with a big club who rides a stegosaurus. It remains a cur-rent theme in the big budget film of 1982, the Fox production of *The Quest for Fire*, titled after the 1921 novel by J. H. Rosney, *The Quest for Fire: A Novel of Prehistoric Times*.[14]

Brion and Lea discover that their troglodytes are not aboriginal, but that they have regressed to the caveman stage owing to their need to adapt to their unprogressive environment, which is dominated by heat- and metal-seeking war machines. (They have been *forced* into primitive stupidity, much like the backcountry Yugoslavians.) This is the team's first clue that the battlefield with its rusted hulks is not a thing of the past. Indeed, signs of ongoing military action, moving tanks and diving fighter planes, have already been noted. The problem now is to find out where they come from—underground factories, or what?

The mystery deepens when Brion comes upon a recently disabled tank, only to find that it has no room for a crew. It is robot-operated. "How can this be possible?" Lea asks. "I thought that robots were incapable of injuring people? There are the robotic laws. . . . " Harrison alludes here to the Three Laws of Robotics formulated by John Campbell and dramatized in the robot stories of Isaac Asimov.[15] Brion replies:

"Perhaps on Earth, but they were never applied out at the fringes of the old Earth Empire. You are forgetting that robots are machines, nothing more. They are not human so we shouldn't be anthropomorphic about them. They do whatever they are programmed to do—and do it without emotional reactions of any kind. They have been used in combat ever since technological warfare began. . . . You'll find that the history of the wars during the Breakdown is filled with references to battles that were almost fully automated." (*Planet of No Return*, chapter 14, my ellipsis)

This is offered in sane rebuttal to all those howling about the dangers of a runaway technology (as if the dish really could run off with the spoon). Technology is just hardware, and when automated with software it will do only what its human programmers have instructed it to do. In a collection of stories given to that lesson (*War with the Robots*, 1962) Harrison points out that robotic machinery at its most complex only extends the design principles of an automatic clock-radio or the first crude models of the automatic pilot.

Brion must now find out who is programming these killer-robots on Selm-II. "They are the real criminals who should be brought to justice" in this "crazy war of robots fighting robots on a virtually uninhabited planet and incidentally shooting up the surviving people at the same time" (chapter 14).

At last Brion finds these war criminals in the penultimate chapter, "Into the Military Mind," at the very source of the machines. They are brought from two other planets by means of matter transmitters (the subject of another Harrison collection, *One Step from Earth*).[16] Remote-control TV cameras beam the war to both homelands, where their publics are limited to watching this entertainment whether they like it or not; and some do not, having tired of "military stupidity." Addressing one side's general, Hegedus, the captured Brion indicates to him the unexpected news that innocent people, the survivors of a mining town, had been reduced to troglodytes by this imported war. "You people have a lot to answer for." In that case, Hegedus concedes, the war on Selm-II will end, and no doubt the natives will benefit when the CRF comes in to clean things up. This conversation ensues:

"Have you benefited as well?" Brion asked. "Do you realize how wasteful and economically insane this endless war has been for your world?"

"You will watch your words!" Hegedus said, angry, losing his composure for the first time. "You sound dangerously like a member of the World Party. Production for consumption not war, more consumer goods, legal unions . . . we've heard it all before. Perverted rot. Anyone who speaks that way is an enemy of society and must be extirpated. The World Party is illegal, its membership confined in labor camps. Armies are freedom, military weakness a crime."

Brion then thinks to himself: "Words are not going to stop these madmen. They actually lived in a military and jingoist idea of heaven. Wave the flag, my country right or wrong, build up armament industries, repeal all civil rights—and go to war forever!" In the end, Brion and Lea are released after they learn that the war is to be transferred to another planet, one hopefully unoccupied this time.

But if war is only the product of a special breed of "military morons," murder is a different crime altogether. In the age of superstition, before the Enlightenment, crime and sin were synonymous. To punish the criminal was to expiate the crime in the eyes of God. The enlightened, however, took the view that personal vengeance is out of order because society itself is the culprit. This view, still part of the liberal heritage, is perfectly expressed by H. G. Wells in a parallel-world novel of socialist science fiction, *A Modern Utopia*: "Crime and bad lives are the measure of a State's failure, all crime in the end is the crime of the community. Even for murder Utopia will not, I think, kill."[17]

Harrison picks up on this idea in "From Fanaticism, or for Reward," part of *One Step from Earth* (1970), a collection of stories about matter transmission (MT). A hired assassin is pursued for twenty years by the Follower, a robot policeman of the Greater Despot. It is quite a chase, from world to world, via a vast MT system of personal transport. But the Follower catches up with him not to kill him, but only to say,

"You are nothing, and the men who hired you are nothing. But why they did it and how they were able to do it is everything. One man, ten men, even a million are as nothing to the Greater Despot who numbers the planets in his realm in the hundreds of thousands. The Greater Despot deals only in societies. Now an examination will be made of your society and particularly of the society of the men who hired you. What led them to believe that violence can solve anything? What were the surround-

ings where killing was condoned or ignored—or accepted—that shaped their lives so
that they exported this idea?

"It is the society that kills, not the individual" (171).[18]

And what fate has the Greater Despot in store for that guilty society? Unprogressive and dead to reason, it is likely destined for burial. Or else it is due for a leveling course of social reconstruction that will punish not the criminal, but all those of wealth and station who incite him to murder, mugging or whatever by the example of their economic violence in the competition for gain, not to say by envy. The right to provoke crime and bad lives is no right. Again, as Harrison says, his villains are not really villains because they are *forced* to do evil. So why not force wicked societies to be good?

Skeptical Tales

Of course, crime as a sin cannot be avenged if there is no God. Harrison's one explicitly aetheistic story is "The Streets of Ashkelon" which, hard to believe in these days of freedom from religious censorship, he had trouble getting published back in 1961, after five to six years of rejection. The title refers to the Second Book of Samuel in the Old Testament. David has come upon the smiter of Saul and his son Jonathan, who says, "I have slain the Lord's annointed." David laments: "Thy glory, O Israel, is slain upon the high places! How are the mighty fallen! Tell it not in Gath, publish it not in the streets of Ashkelon; lest the daughters of the Philistines rejoice, lest the daughters of the uncircumcised exult" (2 Samuel 1: 16, 19–20). In other words, the spiritually impure, or heathens of Ashkelon, might rejoice to hear that two of the Lord's chosen have been slain. In the story, a Christian missionary to Wesker's World is asked to demonstrate the truth of what he preaches regarding the doctrine of the Lord's death and resurrection. He quite unwillingly obliges, is crucified, buried, and does not rise on the third day. The Weskers, pure in nature and among whom murder is unknown, are disappointed. Now they will not be saved. But they had nothing to be saved from, and now they have become murderers. How the Philistines will rejoice in the killing of that hapless missionary, with its affirmation of their sufficiency without the Word.

But even the verities of reason have their limits, when the reasonable men of science come into their own established authority. That is the burden of "Toy Shop," in which a small group of physicists have found a minor slip in Newton's laws. So unorthodox is this discovery that they have been forced underground; no industrial laboratory will research and develop their scale model of a lift-propulsion device that works on new principles that will make pure space flight possible. Their working model cannot as yet lift its own weight, but it has potential, given a big enough R & D investment. But the scientific establishment will have nothing to do with it. The renegade scientists then sell it as a plaything in a toyshop near a large industrial lab. Its demonstrator sells it as the Atomic Wonder Space Tapper, and the pitch is, it hangs on space waves. This toy catches the fancy of one of the local lab technicians, who buys it for the sole purpose of spoofing his kids with the same sales pitch. He of course was expected to be wise to the evident trickery involved, as he smugly noted the black thread used to elevate the demonstration model, and as he laughed inwardly at the "dummy" coils that supposedly gave the toy its lifting power by tapping the energy of gravity waves. But in pretending to be fooled, for the sake of the purchase, he really was fooled in a more sophisticated way. What he did not know, when he took this toy home for the delight of his children, was that the thread attached to it was calculated to break just as the toy was lifted a few inches off the floor, *unless* the "dummy" coils, not fake at all, were electrified per the enclosed instructions. The children would read these and then show their father that the Atomic Wonder Space Tapper did indeed have the power to float in the air without the aid of any thread. *That* would grab his attention!

Chapter Four
Conceptual Breakthrough

This chapter is given over to one outstanding novel, *Captive Universe* (1969). To explain why the work is exceptional and deserving of singular attention, I do not hesitate to back off quite a distance to lead into it.

Every college student learns how wonderful was the Renaissance and its revival of learning, and how magnificent were those Renaissance men who led medieval Europe out of the Dark Ages. After this progressive prelude to we happy moderns, the student will be excused if he inclines to think of the Enlightenment as but a postscript to the Renaissance.

Yet the Age of Reason so differs from what went before, regarding knowledge and learning, that without it a certain type of science fiction would be inconceivable. The Renaissance is responsible for the Faustian version of the Tree of Knowledge taboo. Although challenged by the later rationalists, it survives to this day in occult science fiction and dominates science fiction in the cinema. It was Marlowe, Shakespeare's contemporary, who stated the case for this irrational theme in the gushy Chorus to *The Tragical History of Doctor Faustus*:

> Faustus is gone: regard his hellish fall,
> Whose fiendful fortune may exhort the wise,
> Only to wonder at unlawful things,
> Whose deepness doth entice such forward wits
> To practice more than heavenly power permits.

But poor Faust was interested only in gold, girls, and guns, not in supernal learning for its own sake.

Boris Karloff said it better in the film *The Invisible Ray* (1936): "There are some things Man is not meant to know."[1] Karloff was playing a chastened mad scientist in this Universal Pictures horror film that continued the tradition begun with the studio's production of *Frankenstein* (1931). Its hero is punished for his quest for knowledge that goes against the will of God; its piety is little more than a Renaissance relic.

Indeed, the legend of Doctor Faustus lives on in so great a part of modern science fiction (all of technophobic science fiction) that some critics name

Mary Shelley's 1818 novel *Frankenstein* as the source of the whole genre. Moreover, so much of social science fiction is dystopian that one critic holds the opinion that science fiction is typified by the future-as-nightmare theme.[2] If these judgments are correct, they place the bulk of the genre with "modern" liberalism's mistrust of science and technology, in a betrayal of the Enlightenment.

But where enlightened science fiction prevails, one of its most important themes is the "conceptual breakthrough." This tags a type of story in which a quest for knowledge leads to the discovery of a new state of reality. Apparent certainties are questioned by a nonconformist seeker, and the world turns out to be wildly different from what it seems to be.[3]

Robert Heinlein's "Universe"

In Robert Heinlein's "Universe," a famous example, the world turns out to be a starship on a mission of many generations. But its mission—to colonize a planetary system light years from Earth—and guiding scientific culture have collapsed; and with that breakdown, the Dark Ages have returned. Everybody aboard the ship now thinks of it as their complete universe; no one understands that it is a mode of transport moving through the larger universe of stars unseen outside. The hero, unsatisfied with the world-myth taught him, seeks his own answers and eventually finds the stars, as viewed from the ship's long unmanned control room. But his truth fails to persuade, and, like Galileo, he is tried for heresy, uttering at the end the same words: "Nevertheless—it [Earth/the ship] *still* moves!"

For the enlightened, Galileo's trial was a perfect object lesson in medieval superstition and churchly stupidity, and it remains so for modern day rationalists. So important were Galileo's alleged words to the cause of truth-seeking that they in fact were not spoken by him but were invented for the sake of a higher verity. They are the "pious fraud" (a Jesuitical phrase) of the anticlerics. Moreover, the grounds of Galileo's trial for heresy were not his Copernican astronomy per se, but its unscientific and cultish use as an ideological cover story on the part of some very real heretics (Galileo not among them) who in fact were conspiring against the order of the existing church-state. The real question, concealed in the language of the trial's legal double-talk, had to do with a case of subversion of the sort peculiar to theocratic power politics.[4]

The Galileo case offers a complicated basis for an interesting story in the field of political science fiction, in which the opponents on both sides, churchmen and scientists alike, are perfectly rational. But it does not have the dramatic simplicity of science and theology engaged in a contest for the victory of progress and truth over barbarism and lies.

In the Heinlein story, the hero who has come upon astrophysical truth is brought to trial by those among the ship's officers called scientists, as once upon a time they in fact were, but now they have regressed to medieval scholasticism and a new kind of geocentric fallacy. So the hero's conceptual breakthrough is lost upon them, and the ship's mission seems fated to be forever forgotten.

"Universe" was published in John W. Campbell's ASF in 1941, and caused excitement because readers recognized that Heinlein had created a new science fiction idea, something almost unheard of after H. G. Wells alone seemed to have invented (where he did not carry forward) every narrative subject in the field. In this case it was the idea of the generation starship, as the motif is indexed in science fiction encyclopedias. Thereafter until it became stale, almost every writer in the business tried his hand at this fresh idea, in an effort to solve the problem Heinlein failed to solve—even if his not solving it was part of the story. The problem, simply stated, is how to get a closed society of colonists to their destination without untoward culture change over the many generations it takes to get there. In "Universe," the society breaks down following a mutiny. So the question for the writers after Heinlein was how to design safeguards against instability.

Harrison's Solution

Then in 1969 came Harrison's *Captive Universe*, with an answer so different, so novel, so downright astonishing, as to remake the original story idea into something else altogether. Indeed, *Captive Universe* transcends not only the narrative subject, but the science fiction genre itself; or so Gilbert Highet thought in strongly recommending it as a Book-of-the-Month Club selection for April 1969. He concluded his review by saying, "the book is not merely space-fiction but also religious allegory."

Religious allegory? It is hardly that, but never mind. It *is* what I believe to be Harrison's literary masterpiece. And if it be more than mere space-fiction, it is because *Captive Universe* is a work of refined literature, in which form and content, evocative language and subdued intelligence, are united with polished artistry. Its plot, as a fantastic solution to a problem only science fiction fans recognize, is not in the least relevant to this higher judgment.

If I give the solution here, it is only to advise the reader that the novel is to be appreciated apart from that; it is but the starting point for an original work of superior imagination. Perhaps that is what Highet meant by describing it as a religious allegory. But so far as the starship question is concerned, the answer is an eponymous Designer who has installed a painfully ascetic order of priests and nuns as the crew to secretly supervise the colonists, whose loyalty is to an even more superstitious religion. The Designer's aim is to maintain in the ship a conservative social order, under the oppression of a religious faith so primitive and stupid that no culture change can affect this human machinery designed for stability and continuity until the mission is completed. But not even the crew (ascetic save for dutiful reproduction) knows what the mission is.

Gilbert Highet commences his review of *Captive Universe* cautiously because it is the first science fiction novel to be promoted by the Book-of-the-Month Club and it competed with, of all titles, *The Godfather* by Mario Puzo:

You will either enjoy this fantastic story very much indeed or be unable to finish it. Two readers whose judgment I respect merely laughed when I tried to discuss it seriously [the nonserious view of science fiction that Auberon Waugh once prided himself in]; two others confessed to having been haunted by it for weeks. It begins in an Aztec village, apparently pre-Columbian in date, dominated by a grim priesthood and terrorized by dreadful deities who appear in person. The first chapter, in which the snake-headed goddess Coatlicue hunts down a victim and tears out his heart, is what publishers irreverently call a Grabber.[5]

But I will not give that away! Soon it becomes evident that these Aztecs are not altogether the ones we know from anthropology; a few little things are wrong with them—blond hair? blue eyes? And what about those written books and iron knives?

The story's young hero, Chimal, becomes a rebel, lonely intellectual type that he is, disposed to curiosity. He determines to break the law of the land by exploring the mountain walls that ring his valley and keep his and a neighboring village from any outside contact. After many fearful adventures that do not deter him, Chimal finds his way through the mountain barrier, where he penetrates not into another valley, but into another world. This is a world of elaborate and advanced machinery, served by dedicated technicians dressed in black religious habits. The technology described is as far ahead of what we today know as the Aztecs are behind it. Chimal explores this world, only to find that the very sun moving overhead is part of its mechanism, and that he can walk the dome of the sky, from rim to rim, while looking down on his distant village far below. All such crazy wonders are described with inerrant plausibility, for what Chimal discovers is that both the technocrat priests and his own "Aztec" community inhabit the inside of a cavernous planetoid, hollowed out five centuries earlier by the Designer. He peopled it with "Aztec" peasants, his colonists, and obedient, self-perpetuating servants of the machinery. They are all passengers and crewmen on a vast spaceship, outward bound to a particular star, light years away, around which circles a planet on which the colonists will settle at journey's end. Meanwhile they are content to continue their limited lives, generation after generation, with the pious crew dedicated to service, and the "Aztecs" dedicated to fear of the gods and despair. But all this was worth it, for the Designer has not only programmed the artificial Aztec culture and the religious culture of the crew to be both stable and unchanging; he has also programmed, through genetic engineering, the final emergence of the savior genius, Chimal. He emerges at the right time with the right combination of chromosomes from the two villages, given the original selection, in accord with the working out of the law of exogamy. As planned, he is endowed with the intelligence to make a conceptual breakthrough and achieve a scientific understanding of the mission—whose operating manuals he duly seeks out and finds.

In the end he directs the asteroid, a vast flying prison, to its proper destination, and renews the lives of its prisoners. Programmed enlightenment follows programmed suffering and oppression!

Some reviewers have named the Designer a mad scientist, an evil genius. I disagree, of course, as my previous chapters on Harrison's work and his place in the genre indicate. If not a religious allegory, perhaps then *Captive Universe* is a political allegory, arising from those conflicting ideals of freedom and power expressed elsewhere; but nowhere else is that ideological tension transmuted into such pure artistry as in this work, readable at more than one level of meaning.

Chapter Five
Make It New!

Harrison has followed Ezra Pound's famous advice in a field where true novelty is difficult to achieve and often not even expected. There are a number of themes, largely set by H. G. Wells, that the science fiction writers play upon, dear old themes the fans love to hear retold over and over again. In this respect, the genre is not unlike the oral tradition of the Eskimo storyteller, who delights his audience with the same set of familiar stories, his art resting with the ability to retell them with interesting variations.

In this chapter, the narrative themes are time-travel and parallel worlds, both related by some jiggery-pokery with the fourth dimension, treated either as the dimension of time itself or as an extended dimension of space. Wells's *Time Machine* (1895) introduced the former theme and his *Modern Utopia* (1905), with its alternate Earth, the latter, although the latter can be traced back to an earlier short story, "The Remarkable Case of Davidson's Eyes" (1895), where a man's vision and his body occupy two different spatial worlds.

Harrison's ability to "make it new!" lies with the freshness of his variations, whereas in other hands they are less fresh than repetitive unto staleness. In addition—and here is where the sense of novelty really springs from—he but *uses* the narrative subject at hand to load it with information of topical and didactic interest quite apart from reworking the ins and outs of time-travel, or whatever, for its own thematic sake. Thus, while only science fiction fans may recognize the elegance of the variation, readers unacquainted with the genre are in for a good read, irrespective, and for an educational experience as well.

The Hollywood Vikings and
The Technicolor Time Machine

The Technicolor Time Machine (1967), serialized the same year in ASF (March, April, May) as "The Time Machined Saga," is a work of comic genius. The business of Hollywood movie-making and the Viking sagas are mixed together in one story, both treated with refreshing insight.

I asked Harrison if he had in mind at any point the story by P. Schuyler

Miller, "As Never Was," from the January 1944 issue of ASF. He said the novel was in fact a play on that story in one particular; the bottle of Jack Daniels in the one is meant to recall the unearthly knife of present and future in the other. The Miller story was the first tale since Wells's *Time Machine* to introduce a new twist called, as Harrison phrased it, "the no beginning, no end paradox." "As Never Was" tells the story of an archaeologist who, using a time shuttle, digs up a knife in some ruins of the distant future and brings it back for a museum erected in his name; his grandson, hoping to learn about the culture that produced the knife (perhaps an alien colony?), revisits the site only to find the ruins of his grandfather's museum. The knife has no beginning, no end; it exists in a closed loop.

That story, and subsequent variants, is limited in its plot to the working out and revelation of this particular paradox of time-travel. But the bottle of Jack Daniels in *The Technicolor Time Machine*, when its remains are paradoxically found in the rubbish heap of a Viking settlement at L'Anse aux Meadows in Newfoundland, the probable location of the Vinland of the Icelandic sagas,[1] is but one comic detail in a vastly convoluted and convulsing story about Hollywood on location—in time and space—as it shoots a hoked-up version of Thorfinn Karlsefni's settlement of Vinland.

The funny business begins when the head of Climactic Studios, in the interest of cheaper productions using nonunion labor, resolves his financial problems by sending a crew back in time to shoot the proposed film. They can take as long as they need, so long as they bring back a completed film by the weekend, when his bank intends to foreclose on him. For this purpose he had been taken to visit a laboratory (looking to him like "an old set for *Frankenstein*") belonging to a Professor Hewlett, who there demonstrates the needed device. "My vrematron—from *vreme*, the Serbo-Croatian for 'time,' in honor of my maternal grandmother who was from Mali Losinj—is a workable time machine" (chapter 1). The humor of this scene arises from disconformity with the usual technical locutions used by science fiction writers to fancy up the by now banality of their nomenclature for the time machine as a standard piece of furniture. Furthermore, in answer to the archetypical question, "But tell me, Professor, how does it work?" the professor answers, "[Y]ou could not possibly understand"; his response is a joke on the whole pulp tradition with its long, technical explanations concerning methods of time-travel.

So the story moves on, with no stage magician's patter, as the crew gets down to business in the Greenland of about A.D. 1000, where it hires a local Norseman called Ottar to play the part of Thorfinn Karlsefni, but only after he is persuaded to play the part for the only payment he will accept: an un-

limited supply of Jack Daniels. As he pushes off in his longship, the crew
travels to Newfoundland to await the arrival of the first Vikings in America.

Harrison's ethnography of Viking culture is faultless, though also ribald
and irreverent. And so is his reading of the two medieval documents in question, the *Grænlendinga Saga* and *Eirik's Saga*. For it turns out in the end
that Ottar really *is* Thorfinn Karlsfeni. And after he returns home to Greenland and the crew returns in time to modern Hollywood, with the film in the
can and the studio saved, Professor Hewlett is consulted on the paradox, but
he does not see why anyone is concerned. "But the significance, Professor, the
significance," he is exhorted to explain, for "If this is true, the only reason that
the Vikings settled in Vinland is because we decided to make a motion picture showing how the Vikings settled in Vinland." His calm reply is, "It's as
good a reason as any other" (chapter 18). So much for paradoxical paradoxes!
Then a closer study of *Eirik's Saga* reveals that all the doings of the crew
while on location in Newfoundland can be interpreted in its light.

As a final twist, archaeologists at L'Anse aux Meadows are reported
shortly thereafter to have uncovered a Viking settlement, which the reader
knows to be none other than the remains of the location crew's camp. The archaeologists are troubled by one find in a midden heap: fragments of a glass
bottle of bourbon whisky—one of many emptied by Ottar.

The Technicolor Time Machine, like all of Harrison's novels, is an adventure story. It is characterized by a sense of great romping fun, with nothing
ideological and nothing serious apart from the load of instructive content that
it easily carries regarding two things unrelated yet wittily juxtaposed in a
most attention-getting way: the movie business and Viking culture. But, as
Harrison says, he always uses the adventure format because "it can be used to
disguise anything."

The theory behind his remark is that in a good story, whatever it is
about, "something always moves at some level." That, in fact, he says, is
Hemingway's dictum on the matter. And, because he writes what he likes
to read, which is the adventure novel, he finds in that format the movement
useful to cover all his varied purposes. In the adventure story, "the something that always happens is the action, the dialogue, and the change of
scene." Moreover, if at moments of high didacticism he "slows down the story
for a lecture, he must have an interesting mode to do it in," which only the
novel-length adventure format can supply; so that the impatient reader,
eager to get on with the action, "may enjoy the novel at the story level
alone," recognizing the slowdowns for what they are in a linear narrative of
unfailing movement. He compares this technique to that of the platform
speaker who "uses jokes in his lecture, the audience waiting for the next

joke." Only with the novel, it is the reader who is waiting for the next line of happening.

Rebel in Time

Rebel in Time (1983) uses the adventure format and time-travel to a deadly serious purpose. As Harrison explains; "I had for years been thinking about a parallel-world, Civil War novel, and so went swimming in the technology of the early 1860s—guns, ships, etc. The Sten-gun in the book is very simple to make without gunsmiths. I read an article about copies of it being made by the Resistance Movement [in Europe during World War II]. This was the gun for my novel; with it, the South would win the war. Then I needed only a rotten Southerner for a villain."

The "rotten Southerner" is the bigoted, redneck Colonel McCulloch, "old Snarly" to his fellow servicemen, who hates blacks and uses the N word. But wait—has not Harrison repeatedly said that there are no villains in his books, but that they are *forced* to be evil by "social forces" and the like? In this case, the social force is racism; the colonel is the product of a wicked society, just a hapless puppet of racist culture. No devil figure, then, to be indicted for personal crimes, he therefore can be killed off in the name of avenging social justice. Indeed he is killed by Sergeant Troy Harmon who, in contrast to him, is moved by a sense of moral obligation on an individual ethical basis, as the good guys must be if the impersonal forces of evil are to be defeated.

Sergeant Harmon is black, seconded from the military service to serve as a secret agent in a rarefied security operation given to watching over lesser operatives. The security service is now interested in the colonel because after the sale of stock holdings he has amassed forty-nine pounds of gold worth a quarter of a million dollars. Harrison says he would not have presumed to write a black hero into this novel if "I did not understand something of black middle-class thinking. For the character of Troy Harmon, not wanting him to be two-dimensional, I have drawn upon those black artist friends who worked with me in my comic factory, after having gone to school together. I also recalled to mind a close friend I worked with during the war. So I felt that I could handle this character in a believable way."[2]

As the story develops, Colonel McCulloch goes back in time to just before the outset of the Civil War, taking with him his gold, and also a copy of the Sten-gun and its blueprints lifted from the Technological Archives of the United States Army. He time-travels by making unauthorized use of the Gnomen project at Weeks Electronic Laboratory Number Two, a secret government laboratory where "Old Snarly" had served as chief of security.

Harmon (the only one to speak of "a working time machine," so domesticated is the device by the adventure story plotted around it) figures this out,
and follows him. Harmon's cunning ways, as a black man in the antebellum
South, in pursuing his mission of vengeance are a remarkable part of the
story. At last he catches up with the colonel, who is working for his cause by
manufacturing the Sten-gun in Hall's Rifle Works at Harper's Ferry, just on
the eve of John Brown's raid. Harmon kills the colonel with a pistol shot as
the raid begins, and as McCulloch lays dying, is amazed to learn of the raid.
John Brown would have scotched the colonel's cause if Harmon had failed.
As it turns out, the colonel (not a very bright student of history anyway) had
brought with him as a guide to events the only book on the Civil War that
does not mention the raid on Harper's Ferry: Fletcher Pratt's *Ordeal by Fire*.[3]

Under cover of the raid, Harmon burns down the rifle works, where crates
of the Sten-gun are stacked. With the colonel's gold, he organizes a battalion
of Negro regiments which he leads into crucial battles from the start of the
war. Neither of these events happened in the history we know—nothing was
destroyed at Harper's Ferry, and Negro volunteers were not organized by the
North until late in the war. An alternate world has come into being, thanks to
Sergeant Harmon's trip into the past, to change the history books of the future from which he came. He learns all about these changes from his white
girlfriend, a technician with the Gnomen project, who now loves him all the
more for the dangers he has passed. She brings with her the record of his battle deeds, but he alone knows the difference between the two worlds, based
on his recollection of the old history he read in books before his mission to
chase down the colonel and the new history of the South's loss that he had
helped to shape. But Harmon, now a sergeant-major in the Union Army,
shares that knowledge with her as they face life together in the war's closing
year of victory.

Quite apart from masterful storytelling and an authentic black hero, *Rebel
in Time* delights by playing against the expectations of a whole subgenre of
"what-if-the-South-had-won-the-war?" novels, whose premier and classiest
example is Ward Moore's *Bring the Jubilee* (1953). Another favorite "what
if" subject is Allied defeat in World War II, exemplified in top form by Philip
K. Dick's *The Man in the High Castle* (1962). Unlike *Rebel in Time*, however, these two novels are of a type that do not depend for their alternate
worlds on the paradoxical effects of time-travel. Rather, they assume in the
reader a knowledge of real events, postulate a decisive turning point somewhere in history that leads to a different outcome—the South wins the Civil
War or the Axis powers triumph over the Allies—and ask what would the resulting world look like?

All of the above are variants on the parallel world theme, which Harrison sorted out in his lecture "Worlds beside Worlds" given at the Institute of Contemporary Arts.[4] Type A, in his classification, presumes an infinite number of parallel worlds in the present, with the story based on a visit to one or more of them in a machine that moves, not into the past or the future, but sideways in time between these coexisting worlds. Type B is a simpler sort that deals with a single parallel world of the present, actually an alternate world, as in *Bring the Jubilee*; it is parallel only so far as the real world coexists in the mind of the reader. Complications with type B arise when time travel is introduced as a way of altering the past so as to make for the different outcome in question. Sergeant Harmon does this in *Rebel in Time*, but only to a small extent; his lady love still is the same one he left behind in a world unaltered save for a few historical records of the Civil War.

Tribulations of a Transatlantic Tunnel Builder

Harrison's own working of an uncomplicated variety of type B, *A Transatlantic Tunnel, Hurrah!* (1972), is a comic masterpiece.[5] Its freshness, of course, owes everything to the winning ways of the parallel world Harrison has chosen to imagine, as revealed in the good humor and sheer vigor of the storytelling. What he offers is an amusing affirmation of all the basic ideals and decencies to be found in the Victorian novel, but recast into a wildly mixed contemporary setting.

The "what if" that Harrison posits as the great turning point in history is the defeat of the Christian armies at the battle of Nava de Tolsa in 1212. Surely he must have counted on this choice alone to be humorous for the ahistorical minds of most readers. How could a crazy event that nobody ever heard of change the world so much? But the result of the battle is that Spain and Portugal surrender to Moslem conquerors, Columbus never discovers America (Cabot does—but later), and the American colonies lose their war for independence and remain part of the British Empire. On the European continent, Germany produces no Bismarck and so remains divided into warring principalities, while in France, no Jacobin Revolution shakes the royal throne.

In England—merry olde England!—fatherly aristocrats of faultless lineage remain in the ascendency. English currency is not vulgarized by going decimal, yet railroad locomotives are nuclear powered. Stranger still, airplanes are great, hulking "airships" weighing one hundred tons and driven by coal power! These latter, Harrison tells me, really can fly in a clumsy sort of way; he worked out the calculations with glee, and the engineering details are lovingly described for the technophilic fun of it: giant turboprop engines burning pulverized coal, with the aid of butane gas to start the turbine blades until they come up to sufficient heat and pressure to combust this other unlikely fuel. Still, that system alone won't get these hulks airborne (to save the weight of an immense undercarriage they take off and land on water like a flying-boat), so designed into the tail assembly is a two thousand pound horsepower turbine serving to increase the flow of air over the wings, just barely adding enough lift to fly at all of fifty miles an hour.

The convoluted plot begins with a scheme to build a transatlantic tunnel, running from the Azores to the Grand Banks of Newfoundland, for high-speed trains moved by means of linear traction engines in a vacuum. The engineer best qualified to supervise the whole venture is an American, Captain Augustine Washington. This in spite of the fact that he is a descendant of the traitor George Washington (the story allows him children), shot by the British after he lost the Battle of Lexington. Captain Washington's fondest hope is that his performance might help convince Her Majesty to grant America dominion status—if not independence. He also has romantic hopes of winning the beautiful Iris, daughter of Sir Isambard Brassey-Brunel, the English father of the tunnel scheme (the name echoes that of Isambard Kingdom Brunel, England's greatest engineer who, in fact, as Harrison pointed out to me, had designed a full-scale model of a vacuum-powered railway).

Captain Washington's greatest technical feat is his workable answer to the problem that brought the project to a halt even as it was being planned: how to cross the Mid-Atlantic Ridge. Brassey-Brunel's impractical answer was to go hundreds of miles around it. Washington's astonishing solution, a mile long underwater bridge across the Rift Valley in the Ridge, arouses Brunel's jealousy, and he refuses the captain permission to woo his daughter. Both are made unhappy, but Iris, a proper girl certain of what is right, cannot leave her father because she is all he has; and the captain, courteous and chivalrous in his passion for Iris, also submits. Captain Washington is further troubled by sabotage attempts by the wicked French, adding yet more dangers to the construction process itself, whose engineering details are always depicted with expertise.

But in the end Victorian values earn their just reward, which is why Auberon Waugh in his review confessed, "I cried like a baby at the wedding between the beautiful, good Iris and brave Captain Washington." And that is why Waugh's next and concluding line reads, "It is a book which I can recommend with all my heart." While Harrison is pleased enough with this review to have inserted it as the introduction to a reprint edition of the novel, he estimates that Waugh evidently loved it for the wrong reason: "I wrote it as a comedy, but he took it as a Tory Utopia!"

Education through Time-Travel

One Harrison short story, among others appropriate for this chapter,[6] will serve to conclude because it neatly returns us to an actual experiment carried out by the father of all time travel stories. H. G. Wells in 1895 (the year *The Time Machine* was published) was called upon by a maker of scientific instruments, Robert Paul, who had just perfected his Theatrograph, the first motion picture projector (not well remembered because limited to private projections). But Paul did not know what to film with it for a suitable demonstration project. So Wells wrote him a photoplay, suitable for what he himself viewed as a genuine time machine. The demonstration project (never carried out) was to present the evolutionary drama of planet Earth, from nebula to solar system to the rise of *Homo sapiens* and beyond. Wells envisioned stop-motion photography, dissolves, and other advanced techniques; combining artwork with small models of dinosaurs and cavemen; and a futuristic set the audience could get up to walk about in before returning to their own seats and, on screen, their own time. For Wells, this real, cinematic time machine was a device useful to the teaching of a cosmic perspective on mankind.[7]

In "The Ever-Branching Tree" (1969), Harrison relates the use of time-travel as a regular teaching aid at the gradeschool level. A teacher takes her young pupils back to the origins of life and up through all the vital branching points in the Darwinian tree of life, returning to the classroom by dismissal time. The story offers a good, compact lesson in evolutionary biology—Harrison in the high didactic mode—but is relieved by the children's amusing reactions. For them, a time machine has no more magic than today's audiovisual aids, whose reels of topical matter descend from the world's first instructional film, scripted by H. G. Wells as an adventure in time traveling.

Chapter Six
Humor and Parody
Parodying Heinlein

The two words in this title go together because they designate works by Harrison that induce humor by parodying works written by other science fiction writers. *Bill, the Galactic Hero* (1965), as Harrison carefully explains, is an example of "black humor" directed as "black satire" against the military, and at the same time is a "parody" of a novel sympathetic to military life. His choice of language is exactly right. Satire takes for its province the morals and manners of some institution, with the view to amending its wicked ways by means of accentuating them; and the degree of blackness the readership will be amused by depends on how deeply it harbors the prejudices it shares with the satirist. To parody the work of another is to imitate the original by combining an amusing mixture of likeness and unlikeness, the success of the intended humor depends on the reader's recognition of this mix and again on how sympathetic he is with the parodist's motive.[1]

Bill, the Galactic Hero parodies the enormously popular *Starship Troopers* (1960), written by Robert A. Heinlein, who did not enjoy Harrison's joke. His own reserved displeasure, however, little reflected the "immortal storm" that brewed up over it, dividing fans and writers alike. Many were not amused by the taking in vain of the soon-to-be Grand Master's name,[2] nor by the blackening of the American military, as implied in the novel's caricature of the Vietnam War through Helior's imperial war against the harmless little lizard-like Chingers. In the midst of this controversy, nobody bothered to inveigh against Helior, at another level of meaning, as a travesty of Trantor, the planet-wide city covered in metal that lies at the heart of Isaac Asimov's galactic empire in his "Foundation" series, begun for ASF from 1942 and collected in an omnibus volume, *The Foundation Trilogy* (1964); Asimov unlike Heinlein, was pleased to be parodied.

Still, Harrison's *Bill* sold very well and has been reprinted as one of a handful of classics in the Avon Science Fiction Rediscovery series (1975). Its reputation is deserved because it brims over with zany twists on nearly every possible science fiction cliché from the genre's history. One comic focus of interest that in reality is not so laughable is the problem of disposing of disposable products; plastic trays are mentioned thirty-seven times (by my count) as a running joke in one of the novel's insanely paced subplots. The ideological tone of the parody's address to its chief target is exemplified in the following comparison with the original.

Starship Troopers tells the story of Johnnie Rico, who works his way through the service ranks of the Terran Federation until he qualifies for the Mobile Infantry (M.I., akin to the Marine Corps only with more mobility and firepower), whose mission is to strike the forward bases of the collectivist Bugs (a rival superpower of the twenty-second century). The hero of *Bill, the Galactic Hero* is just plain Bill, enrolled in a correspondence course for a career as Technical Fertilizer Operator down on the farm, until a recruiting robot cons him into joining the Imperial Space Troopers with visions of bright nebular lights, jazzy red uniforms—and a cup of deep-space knockout drops. Bill wakes up aboard the Empire space ship *Christine Keeler* (named after the mistress who figured in the resignation of John Profumo, British secretary of war, on 5 June 1963), where the officers live in drunken, air-conditioned luxury, while the troopers are sent to the swampy surface of the planet of the Chingers, there to fight against the Empire's hapless enemy. No esprit de corps here, as in the M.I., only oligarchic cruelty.

By an act of accidental heroism, Bill wins the Purple Dart Medallion and an all-expenses-paid trip to Helior, the fabulous, aluminum-plated Sin City of the Empire. While there, his past catches up with him (sleeping on duty), and he is thrown into a prison before being shipped out again. To avoid trouble from the sergeant on guard, Bill points to the ribbon and medal on his chest and lies, "I got that by killing thirteen Chingers singlehandedly in a pillbox I had been sent into. I got into this here stockade because after killing the Chingers I came back and killed the sergeant who sent me in there" (book 3, chapter 2). His remark is a slighting allusion to Private Rodger Young, the infantryman who attacked and died destroying an enemy pillbox in the South Pacific during World War II, and for whom Johnnie Rico's M.I. starship is named.

Harrison says that *Bill* "attempts to blow up the concept of intersteller warfare and galactic empires [in science fiction] once and for all."[3] But a French critic of the genre, pointing to the novel's more obvious theme, puts it on a par with Joseph Heller's *Catch-22* (1961), a grotesque comedy set in a real theater of war, whose title became a catch phrase among its massive, youthful readership during the Vietnam era.[4]

Harrison reports that the publishing success of his own antiwar novel has caused a "literary packager" to come to him with a proposal for a series of six

titles whose action is to take place "in the *Bill* universe." The first of these he
now is writing as I write this, and it features a hero named Jonkarta, after
John Carter of Mars (with a Virginia accent) in the "Barsoom" series of Edgar
Rice Burroughs (from 1912). Harrison discovered Burroughs at the age of
eight, and still finds him a "master of the cliffhanger," even if ignorant of science. The other five books in the series are to be farmed out to one or two
ghost writers, over whom Harrison will hold "editorial control" in the supply
of "the antimilitary theme and a minimum of five hundred words of plot outline [for each title]."

The liberal writer's hostility to military life is quite normal and the reasons
for it are not far to seek. The only remarkable thing about James Burnam's
explanation below is that he troubled to spell it out:

Concepts of equality, non-discrimination and universal democracy are hard to reconcile with the inequalities, authoritarianism, detailed discrimination and rigid hierar-
chy that are always and inevitably characteristic of military organization; even if they
can be reconciled by some sort of complicated logical exercise, there remains a feeling
gap. In his scale of priorities the soldier is professionally committed to place the safety
and survival of his country first, and to be ready to sacrifice his life as well as his freedom and comforts thereto; he must keep the values of social justice and individual
rights secondary in rank, if he is to do his soldierly duty; and his devotion to peace,
however fervently protested, will always be confused by the fact that his trade is war.[5]

The literary tone of *Bill* was defined after the monstrosities of World War I
by antiwar authors, including such brilliant writers as Jaroslav Hasek, in *The
Good Soldier Schweik* (1916–23), Louis-Ferdinand Céline, in *Journey to the
End of the Night* (1932),[6] and Eric Maria Remarque, in *All Quiet on the
Western Front* (1929), in which the poor enlisted man is an Everyman,
civilian-minded and a victim of villainous officers.

But here, now, is a mysterious contradiction. Rejoicing in that first step
onto the surface of the Moon as a giant step for all mankind, Harrison is
pleased to be reminded of the fact that it was "we, the [Science Fiction] people who created the idea that put man there."[7] Yet it was American *military*
pilots who flew that mission; and for the quintessence of the repudiated
"military mind," there are none more animated by ideas of valor and heroism and glory than those pilots whose trade is war of the most spectacular
kind since the days of the cavalry charge—they who fly high-performance
aircraft in battle.

Parodying the Doc Smith Tradition

Rather nostalgic in tone and not bitter is the space-opera parody, *Star Smashers of the Galaxy Rangers* (1973). The craft called for in writing this, Harrison said in our Cornwall interviews, "was to find the dumb pattern, then ginger it up in an intelligent imitation, so that a two-layered meaning is introduced in the reader." At the same time, and this was more of a problem, "the story must appeal to the reader who doesn't know the original; it has to be independent for the reader who doesn't spot the sendup." Some young readers, about ten years old he said, did indeed take it as a straight adventure story, "just for the action, the humor and the exciting sex scenes." (The pulp originals were quite asexual and Harrison exaggerates his own use of sex; always he keeps it under discrete control, just as he moderates "action" short of "gratuitous violence.") Some of the older fans, however, were offended by his "making fun of E. E. Smith." Dear old "Doc" Smith! Harrison read his pulp stories as a boy, when he first fell in love with science fiction. Still, *Starsmashers* "is a parody not only of long dead space opera, but of those who would revive it. Larry Niven et al. are trying to go back to space opera." The example given is Niven's *Ringworld* (1970), and the "et al." refers, I would guess, to Niven and Jerry Pournelle's *The Mote in God's Eye* (1974), and perhaps also to L. Ron Hubbard's doorstop-weighty *Battlefield Earth* (1983).

The "Doc" Smith in question is Edward Elmer Smith, Ph.D. (1890–1965), a working chemist who made his mark on the side as the father of space opera with his "Skylark" and "Lensmen" sequences. He much influenced magazine science fiction in the 1930s and 1940s and kept on writing until his death. Most of his books remain in print. Two titles, *The Galaxy Primes* (1959) and *Spacehounds of the IPC* (1931), are perhaps echoed in that of *Star Smashers of the Galaxy Rangers*. But it is E. E. Smith's first novel, *The Skylark of Space* (1928), appearing in *Amazing* two years after its initial issue, that Harrison responds to with esoteric specificity in his parody. For a content analysis of both, see the review article by Alan Greene in the summer 1986 issue of Paul Tomlinson's fanzine for the Harry Harrison Appreciation Society. Here, the characters and the collection of battles and weird aliens in *Starsmashers* are given their point for point references to the original.[8]

Paul Tomlinson himself, in the same issue, provides a background article on the history of space opera.[9] In the old days of radio, corny domestic dramas were dubbed "soap operas" because they were sponsored by the makers of household products like soap and soap powders. The term was later adapted to corny western stories in the pulps as "horse operas." "The term 'space opera' was originally coined by Wilson Tucker[10] in 1941 for the 'hack, grinding, stinking, outworn spaceship yarn.' These space stories differed little from the westerns—horses were replaced by spaceships, six-guns by ray guns and Red Indians by green bug-eyed monsters."

If Doc Smith invented the genre, its principal developers during the 1920s and 1930s were Edward Hamilton (star smashing adventures about destroying whole worlds and suns) and John W. Campbell in his early "super science" phase. "In the 1940s and 1950s the genre grew less naive, but it continues to today. Several 'Star Trek' episodes owe much to the naiveté of space opera, and [the film] *Star Wars* made space opera popular again in the 1970s and 1980s."

Tomlinson closes on a rather unhopeful note: "Space opera in the pulp magazines gave SF the hardware of rocket ships and ray guns; the square-jawed scientist hero and the dumb-blond girl friend of the hero who faints at the sight of danger, and falls into the evil clutches of the villain/alien so that the hero has to rescue her. To most people this IS science fiction." For Harrison, however, *Star Smashers of the Galaxy Rangers* is at once a campaign to end that kind of outworn science fiction, and an affectionate tribute to E. E. Smith.

Parodying C. S. Forester's Sea Sagas

One other parody takes off on the novels of C. S. Forester, the sea stories that feature Captain Horatio Hornblower. It is a very good-natured and admiring short story titled, "Captain Honario Harpplayer, RN" (1962). Harrison sent a copy of it to Forester with a note stating his intent, that he really meant it in this case when he fell back on the cliché about "imitation being the highest form of flattery." The imperturbable Captain Harpplayer, in command of *HMS Redundant*, is able to accommodate even the landing of an alien space craft and its little green pilot to his true-blue British scheme of things. The tale is a marvel of underplayed humor.

Chapter Seven
Dark Side Up

H. G. Wells invented a genre of nonfiction that his French critic Jean-Pierre Vernier has called "horror sociology," dealing in awful social crises already upon us or about to descend.[1] Its modern practioners like Vance Packard with *The Hidden Persuaders* (1957) and Alvin Tofler with *Future Shock* (1970), have often made the best-seller lists. The works by Harry Harrison treated in this chapter are science-fictionalized horror sociology.

Make Room! Make Room! and Overpopulation

First and foremost in this category is *Make Room! Make Room!* (1966), subtitled "A Realistic Novel of Life in 1999," in which the most ominous trend of all ominous trends in the world has come to the point of irreversible crisis: overpopulation. The setting is a New York City of thirty-five million inhabitants at the turn of the next century, crowded to suffocation and living on a tasteless diet of synthetic food and seaweed crackers. To be sure, there are a lucky or selfish few who live less modestly.

The story revolves around a Chinese teenager who is forced to steal to survive and who is obliged to kill the racketeer-owner of a luxury apartment he breaks into; a detective and riot-control policeman who is assigned to hunt down the killer; the racketeer's mistress, a good girl after all, who is only forced to hustle for a living and who is taken up by the detective to share demurely his apartment, already shared with an old man who remembers the old days. (Indeed, "Room-mates" [1970] is the title of a reworked short-story version that excels in its characterization of Andy the detective and Sol the old man.) The detective serves as the hero because, as Harrison says, his job allows him to act as "a mobile agent through all layers of society," thus showing the reader what the novel really is about, its background, and giving a vivid picture of what the world will be like if its demographic trends are not checked.

That Harrison did his homework on this novel is evident from its bibliography, and I would not challenge the source material save that Paul R. Ehrlich has passed on it in the introduction he wrote for all the paperback reprint editions. Himself a master of horror sociology, Dr. Ehrlich is known for his activism in the Zero Population Growth movement, and he does mention the "population explosion" taking place in Tokyo and Calcutta, but not in New York. That is a significant omission. For the demographic facts were, at the time of the novel's writing, something of a different order. New York City was actually losing population, and all the urban growth in the United States was occurring at the lower and intermediary levels of what sociologists call the rank/size pyramid, in which rank times size equals a constant. Indeed, most of the increased rate of urbanization was accounted for by the numerous small towns that, now widening the base of the pyramid (the constant remaining constant), had grown sufficiently large to meet the minimum definition of a city as defined by the Census Bureau—which reported an overall demographic decline. So, the "population explosion" reduces in this case to rapid urbanization at the lower ranks of the rank/size pyramid, but is combined with a general *loss* of population.

This overall trend has not changed. Last year (1987) the birth rate was down to 1.7, which means that the country is not even replacing itself. For Harrison to play on the horrors of overpopulation at the same time he elsewhere places emphasis on freedom from religion and received ethical standards is contradictory; for the consequences of cultural license have worked against the family as a protector of the birth rate. Indeed, the enlightened, nonmoralistic policy of the government at all levels, in catering to human rights disconnected from the social authority of church or family has, as other horror sociologists ringing a different set of alarm bells claim, so destabilized family life that the normal outcome of marriage in the United States today is divorce (the rate having passed the 50 percent mark), when there *is* marriage to begin with (one in five births now takes place out of wedlock).[2] Thus it is difficult to reconcile the joint presence of welfare statism and cultural license in America, so far as it goes (and Harrison would say that American liberalism does not go far enough, otherwise he would not have left the country) with an alarmist reading of demographic statistics that signal a crisis of overpopulation.

MGM turned the novel into a big-budget film about cannibalism, *Soylent Green* (1973), with Andy (played by Charlton Heston) hunting down not a forgivable Chinese killer, but the source of those seaweed crackers—which are not made of seaweed at all! They are made of the unburied dead. Andy's roommate, Sol, was played by Edgar G. Robinson in his last role, and there is one moment in their dialogue over breakfast, Harrison told me with justifiable pride, that really hit the book's emotional note because he had had a talk with Robinson about that scene, explained to him what the book was all about, and his performance—departing from the stupid script as Heston followed his lead—made for a moving glimpse into the original concept. For that brief moment there came across a vivid sense of "what went wrong with the world?"

As a case study in Hollywood's misuse of source material, *Soylent Green* is well documented in the variety of Harrison's published reactions.[3] To his knowing indictment of what went wrong with the film, I can add little more than a suggestive thought on how MGM might have served him better. His choice of setting need not have been followed, given the fact that New York and other traditional urban centers already were in demographic decline for a number of reasons, including cost of living. The filmmakers could have made the story more relevant by changing the location to the Sunbelt, as they have done with other stories. Instead, they took the even greater liberty of concocting the sensational mystery of the seaweed crackers. But the very real sense of a population explosion that Harrison dramatizes in the novel is actually taking place in Southern California and Florida, and is also changing the ethnic balance of the country as the Hispanic population increases. How people in these places *feel* about such changes registers as explosive, whatever the national demographic statistics may be, and a film addressing this problem would have been much more in keeping with the novel's original dramatic power.

"A Criminal Act" (1966) is a story that suggests what remedies the state may be forced to take if people do not check their own indiscriminate breeding. A bailiff comes to call on the head of a family to declare their second baby illegal and the father fair game for citizen volunteers ready and resentful enough to liquidate him under the Criminal Birth Act of 1993. Since the father had refused advice from his local birth control clinic, a volunteer has been picked by the police and given the usual twenty-four hours in which to do the job with the weapon of his choice. Since the usual immunities from first-degree murder apply, the assassin's only risk is being shot back at, also permitted under the rules. So he sneaks up on the waiting and well-armed father with a machine pistol (wife and two children cringing in the next room of the tiny apartment) and, being well read in cultural relativism, cannot help discussing the situation before pulling the trigger. "Who commits the crime—society or the man? which of them is the criminal?" The father pleads "Natural Law, the sanctity of life, the inviolability of marriage," his children being the "blessings" of that union. The assassin says, "natural law is manmade and varies with the varieties of religion. Argument invalid." Besides, "Your blessings—and the blessings of the rest of mankind—are consuming this world like locusts." Moreover, he goes on, "You are a social animal and do not hesitate to accept the benefits of society" when it suits you—medicine and food rations as welfare handouts for the children, for example. "But you do not accept planning for your family." Rat-tat-tat! The poor man had to be killed because the selfishness of society allowed population growth to get out of hand. Natural law is not natural; the criminal act is not the gunman's but that of irresponsible family life, and murder is morally and legally forgiven.

Geriatrics and Racism

The horrors awaiting those at the vanishing tip of the population pyramid are foreshadowed with mordant humor in "Not Me, Not Amos Cabot!" (1964). Harry says he had great difficulty, over a period of six years, in placing this story because of its taboo subject: the elderly. I think otherwise. A visceral dealing in life and death generally is the province of any great writer, and here Harrison has excelled himself with more honesty than the market normally can bear—except from established greats like Tolstoy or Faulkner.

Seventy-two year old Amos Cabot receives in the mail a free, two-year subscription to *Hereafter*. Subtitled "The Magazine of Preparedness," it carries quite a bit of glossy advertising for legal, funereal, and mortuary services (burial or cremation). Amos indignantly seeks out the magazine's editor to have this "filthy thing" cancelled. It cannot be done, the editor explains, owing to the economics of such "throw away magazines." "I don't mean that we throw them away, on the contrary they go to very selected subscribers, and we don't make our costs back from subscriptions but from the advertisers' fees." Selection is based on the statistics of life expectancy for persons (like Amos Cabot) of a certain age, background, and condition; and "for our purposes a period of two years is satisfactory," during which the advertising messages will have reached saturation before the subscriber dies. Amos improves his daily regimen so as to beat the odds, and rejoices when the last issue of *Hereafter* is a month behind him and he still is alive. But then the postman brings "The Magazine of Geri-ART-trics," titled *Senility*, with ads for toilet chairs, hemorrhoid cushions, wheelchairs, crankbeds, and helpful articles about learning Braille when eyesight fails. The magazine touts these and other services in its introductory letter, and welcomes the subscriber to the "family" of the senile, promising comfort for the many long, empty years ahead—"what happiness to find a copy in your mailbox every month." But the magazine's morbid salesmanship is only a device that underlines the vital issue: Amos's failure to face up to—as many fear to do—the aging process. No, no—it will not happen to me! "Not me" is a genuinely gutsy story, displaying Harrison at his literary best.

Racial issues are the topic of three stories told from a less authentic point of view. The first, "Mute Milton" (1965), dates itself as belonging to the apocalyptic fervor of the early days of the civil rights movement. A "simple-minded Southern son-of-a-bitch of a sheriff," as Harrison described him to me, violently crushes a fourth-dimensional gadget of some kind made by a boyish black genius the likes of the young Einstein. The title comes from a line in Thomas Gray's "Elegy Written in a Country Churchyard": "Some mute inglorius Milton here may rest" (from stanza 15). But the story falls below critical standards for urbane art. Pain is inflicted and endured, with the existential tragedy of primitive drama.[4] Moreover the white author, like many Jewish intellectuals of the time, has presumed to speak for aspiring blacks as if they, too, were an oppressed minority bursting with intellectual talent and disposed to enter the professions once the formal barriers of prejudice and discrimination were lifted. But as Jonathan Kaufman, a Pulitzer-Prize winning reporter for the Boston Globe says in his new book, *Broken Alliance* (1988), "They [Jewish intellectuals] didn't consider that blacks might be different, that they might come to power in different ways—perhaps, like the Irish had, through politics, slowly seizing power in large cities through mayoral elections and civil service."[5] (The next line in Gray's poem moves from Milton to some stilled politician, Cromwell.)

"By the Falls" (1968) is artistically sound, treating the civil rights problem with symbolic detachment, yet with unmistakable moral passion. A man living by The Falls, and great crashing falls they are, has been observing them for over forty years. He says, on the story's closing note of irony, "if there's one man in the entire world who is an authority on The Falls it is me." A visitor arrives and together they watch, through a round, lens-like window, all sorts of debris come down. At one point they see a frightful shipload of people go over the precipice and down The Falls, and the visitor notes their black skins—and the waters turning red with blood. But the keeper of the watch house is dismissive: "Skin is skin, just skin color." The visitor wants to know more, what is up there above The Falls, atop the cliff? "Can there be a whole world up there of which we live in total ignorance?" Yes, indeed there is! It is part of dual world in which blacks are the only ones in pain and the whites the only ones who hate. This presents the blacks as collective victims (all in one passenger ship) in need of collective justice. The cause of social reform here supplants the demands of the constitutional order for personal accountability, on the unlovely assumption that achievement "lies beyond the ability of individual blacks to attain." So writes Glen C. Loury, professor of political economy at Harvard University's John F. Kennedy School of Government. For those black leaders beholden to the example of patronizing whites, he says, "race, and the historic crimes associated with it, has become the single lens through which to view social experience; the infinite potential of real human beings has been surrendered on the altar of protest. . . . This way lies not the 'freedom' so long sought by our ancestors but, instead, a continuing serfdom."[6]

In "Brave Newer World" (1970), a WASP scientist takes on the responsibility to think and act collectively on behalf of the black minority in a future world of controlled population, where all citizens are bred from stored sperm and ova under the authority of the Genetic Guidance Council. (I write WASP, but the Protestant in that acronym is given by default—no religion is mentioned in the story—since Harrison never would have a Catholic for hero.) He notes a disproportion in the small number of stored black genes (smaller still for those of American Indians, the true Americans), and so takes affirmative action by committing proportional ethnic suicide for his own race by breaking a fair number of bottles labeled with names suggesting Anglo-Saxon donors. The laboratory director catches him out at this criminal sabotage, and he confesses before his like-minded colleagues on the council, "committed human beings" all, dedicated to truth and justice; they all "want the facts to come out." The lab director is pleased with the saboteur's oral testimony, but it will go no further. His worthy colleagues, each one addressing their moral hero of the hour, turn to say, "I never heard you admit guilt." Untruth in a higher cause is not unethical. All then celebrate by eating "cult-food" in Old Town, where oppressed minorities are forced to run ethnic restaurants for a living instead of being chemists in New Town laboratories (where they could break bottles on their own behalf, did not racism bar them from the professional world and limit them to business and political affairs in the neighboring urban world).

Other Dark Topics

"The Ghoul Squad" (1969) treats ambulance chasers in the near future while they go about their business of acquiring fresh parts for organ transplants. "I Always Do What Teddy Says" (1963) rebuts B. F. Skinner's utopian scheme, explained in *Walden Two* (1948), for the conditioning of human conduct against antisocial behavior. The killer in the story finds a way around social conditioning by using as a proxy his own son still in the teddy bear stage. The toy bear itself is a conditioning device installed by the state in every home with children. (Brought up the same way himself, the father's motiveless malignity to alter the device to his purpose is unexplained.) "We Ate the Whole Thing" (1972) is a nasty story, titled from a television commercial evidently emblematic of consumer greed. It tells of the world "drowning in its own pollution and excrement" because American corporations have infiltrated and corrupted the international Pollution-Despoilation Committee. "American Dead" (1970) shows what unwonted freedom, in the absence of gun control laws, white citizens will take upon themselves by the year A.D. 2000 to harrass their neighbors of color. The instruments of racism are now mortars and hand grenades.[7]

"After the Storm" (1985) is Europhilic, if not anti-American. The storm in question, as a father tells his hip, hep, with-it daughter, was a global one that (by implication) "we Americans were responsible for." Even dear old antediluvian dad digs a little something of that. "We survived the crises of the twentieth century [it is now the next century] that wreaked destruction on the rest of the world. But we paid—are still paying—a very high price for this. It is time now that we opened our borders again and rejoined the rest of mankind."

At that point, daughter is way ahead of paranoid daddy, who had suspected their visitor from Ireland (who just that morning stole away from their beachfront home with the sailboat he arrived in) of being a Communist spy. Daughter says, "He was a spy alright. A spy from Europe come to look us over. And I know his reasons, too. He wants to see if we are acceptable to the rest of the human race." And perhaps we will be, if reactionary forces never again rise to overturn the decent forces of enlightened statism (social services instead of war and economic competition) and the permissive freedoms of cultural license already indulged to repletion by daddy's daughter.[8].

Chapter Eight
Random Topicality

Harrison's versatility extends beyond science fiction to a number of other genres whose topicality is identified by the subheads in this chapter. While all of this random assortment makes use of the adventure story format, his inventive skills in adapting it to any purpose he chooses are seen here in new abundance.

Crime Novels

The first two of these, the "Revenge" series, were published under the imprint of the Doubleday Crime Club at the suggestion of its editor, Larry Ashmead. Or at least the first one was godfathered that way. Harrison professes to "hate mysteries" and found himself "unable to write a straight mystery," so he did *Montezuma's Revenge* (1972) as a "send-up thriller." And he liked doing it so much that he wrote a sequel, *Queen Victoria's Revenge* (1974). But these books are far too original to be dismissed as mere spoofs on the genre.

As Harrison explained during our Cornwall interviews, he had no idea where to begin until he was told a joke about the ideal title for a *Reader's Digest* article, "An American Indian Who Worked for the FBI, Shot a Bear, and Found God." That did it, and he was off and running with his charmer of a hero, Antonio Hawkin, born 24 December 1941 on the Coyotero Apache Reservation, White Mountain, Arizona, who was appointed by J. Edgar Hoover himself to serve as the first director of the Book and Souvenir Shop to be opened in the lobby of the Federal Bureau of Investigation Building in Washington, D.C.

Tony holds a B.A. in art history from San Diego State College, served as technician fifth class in the U.S. Army, from 1962 to 1964, and from then until the story's opening, was a Federal employee at the National Gallery, where he managed its bookshop. Enter the solemn FBI man who flicks open his wallet badge (Tony asks to see it again), pulls out a sheaf of papers from an inside pocket, reads Tony's vita (which contains the above information and much else), and tells him he has been chosen for an assignment: "He chose you Himself, at once, as the man most qualified for the position. Not only as a loyal American, but as an American American, one of the original ones, as well as being a member of a minority group." Tony wants to know "what this proposed assignment is." Answer: "It is not proposed at all, approved. He approved it Himself." It is the job at the FBI souvenir shop, but Tony is happy where he is, with the art books he knows. "That is unacceptable. Transfer papers are being drawn up—" Unacceptable! Tony will not be coerced. "I appreciate the offer, but tell J. E. H., thanks a lot, but no thanks." Yet Tony must have something to hide if he turns down such an assignment from Him. Tony thinks over all the parking tickets he has torn up, and meekly yields. His office phone rings, the FBI man grabs it, instantly says the affirmative word, then turns it over to Tony. "You can talk now. You are speaking with *Him.*"

And so is Tony the innocent caught up, like the innocent hero of an Eric Ambler suspense novel, as he goes to work in the souvenir shop, selling gilded FBI badges and framed, hand-tinted photos of J. Edgar. In this new, security-obsessed atmosphere, he begins to suspect that the gushing Jewish girl who is his assistant and who forces herself upon him at lunchtime at the Rumbling Tum diner, must be a spy; "and he also suspected that she wasn't even Jewish, a fake minority informer to gain his confidence as a co-minorityist. Her Yiddish expressions were good, but they could have been taught."

But in time, all is revealed. Tony is taken to a patrolled basement room and introduced to Operation Buttercup, after he identifies the painting in a color slide shown in one momentary, guarded flash. It is *Battle of Anghiari* by Leonardo da Vinci, destroyed during World War II by an Allied bomb that fell on the museum in Capitello, Italy, that housed it. But maybe not— the FBI is investigating leads to someone in the U.S. who is trying to sell that painting. Tony's job is to assess it and determine if it is real or fake. Tony says he is not a specialist, just an art historian, just a shop manager. That is all right; he is now "part of the bunch," and that is all that counts, with a security clearance going back to his days in the service, when he was cleared to use classified manuals for a radar unit called the Mark IX-37G. And the reason for security in Operation Buttercup is to keep the CIA out of it; the FBI will handle this alone, no matter where the case leads.

The case leads to Mexico. Tony and the FBI man fly to Mexico City; at the airport Tony has to help out by talking Spanish to the cab driver. This alarms the bureaucratic, not to say provincial, FBI man, who does not remember this language qualification in Tony's dossier, although it is evident that everyone spoke Spanish as well as English on the reservation where he grew up. He

pontificates, "This is going to have to be looked into on a high level." "Well,"
says Tony, "you can't blame me. I didn't write the dossier and I certainly
don't keep Spanish a secret."

No sooner does Tony close the door to their hotel suite than he finds the
FBI man flat on the floor in his room, butcher knife in the back. A knock on
the door; it is not the police but the bellboy. He makes an artistic appraisal of
the knifing job by way of not caring who did it—500 pesos, please. Tony figures that the killer must have been in hiding waiting for them, then slipped
out unseen. He calls the emergency number of last resort for a CIA man code-
named Rooster, who answers at the *Colonel Glanders Mississippi Pollo Asada*.
He and his crew, on the condition they take over Operation Buttercup, come
over and remove the body, now disguised as a party brought into the hotel in
a wheelchair. Rooster then introduces Tony, *his* art expert now, to a German
in possession of the da Vinci painting, which is for sale on behalf of his "master." Tony is to take a look at it by flashlight in the trunk of a car, while wearing the German's Tyrolean hat as a safe sign to the car's driver. As he opens
the trunk Tony is hit from behind and wakes up among boxes of Zion Salami
in the backroom of a Jewish delicatessen, the front for an Israeli agent who
happens to be a noted Nazi-catcher, in pursuit of the German whose hat
Tony was wearing.

Not knowing what he has gotten into, Tony is returned to the hotel to
find a Mexican police lieutenant waiting in his room, wanting to know
about his association with "foreign agents," which the still less than cosmopolitan Tony takes as a nasty allegation; after all, the man in question is an
American. "Mr. Hawkin, please," explains the lieutenant, "In *this* country
an American *is* a foreigner." Tony grants the point, but denies knowing of
Rooster's "foreign" affiliations.

As the policeman leaves, a man steps out of Tony's closet, the underworld
art dealer and driver of the German's car who has come to find out what happened the night of the aborted meeting. The deal is still on, with one million
dollars wanted for the da Vinci painting. Meanwhile, by way of presenting
his bona fides, the dealer entrusts Tony with the other treasure saved from the
ruins of the Monte d'Capitello Museum, which Tony identifies as "The lost
left panel of the Cellini triptych." He is to test the authenticity of this painting, the *San' Sebastiano*, then return it, and he will be taken to see the *Battle
of Anghiari*. Actually, it is revealed, these two paintings were stolen from the
museum by their Nazi owner just before dynamiting it under cover of the air
raid that supposedly destroyed them, then smuggled with other valuables
into Mexico for safekeeping in a bank vault on behalf of his master, none
other than Hitler, who was to come over to Argentina and gain by them

should the war be lost. But now, explains the dealer, the loyal servant must eat. Yet it develops by story's end, that the aging Hitler *is* living in Argentina; but he turns out to be a fake, the whole charade played out owing to complications in selling the da Vinci painting, which also is a fake except for one corner of it saved from the bombed-out ruins together with the Cellini (the dynamite story itself being a fabrication).

At all events, the Mexican police arrive by elevator on Tony's floor as he escapes down the stairs with the Cellini and the butcher knife, fearing to leave it behind. He jumps aboard a battered local bus titled "La Dulca Vida," crowding himself into "the midst of pushing figures with baskets, dangling squawking chickens, bags of beans, crates of cucumbers" (that for local color), which made its last stop at "the open-ended cavern of a bus terminal, Estrella de Oro, a great sign read over the entrance and this gold star was marked prominently on all the vehicles here" (this to show how Harrison always explains his terms, foreign or technical). Tony takes the first Gold Star bus out of town, which happens to be headed for Acapulco. The police are on watch as he disembarks, and give chase, but he eludes them by ducking into a scuba diving school. Hiding the Cellini in the dressing room, Tony finally disposes of the murder weapon that is not his.

Tony goes to an Italian restaurant and, glowered at by the owner (as he thinks) and other darkened visages, orders a meal of spaghetti and meatballs. He still is being watched as his head drops to the table, moaning (in Harrison's favorite line), "They've . . . drugged the spaghetti!" When he wakes up in a back room, he is interrogated by Italian officers of the Agenzia Terza. . . . And that is just the first sixty-three pages, lightly skipped over.

All the players introduced to this point finally converge in a remote part of Mexico around the fake Hitler, and the wonderful nonsense continues to the end. This is Harry Harrison writing as the relaxed world citizen, full of friendly ethnic jokes, informed local color, and historical oddments, all tied together in a madcap adventure story. The same formula animates the sequel, *Queen Victoria's Revenge* (1974), in which the code word "Onion Bagel" puts Tony Hawkin, American Indian FBI agent, in touch with an Israeli commando unit at Cohn's Fancy Bakery in London, whose interest in a bunch of fanatical Scots patriots is the mystery to be unfolded. (Tony never shoots a bear nor finds God, however.)

Also something of a mystery is why Harrison, who does not like mysteries, ghosted a "Saint" novel for Leslie Charteris, *Vendetta for the Saint* (1986). But it came about as follows, Harrison explained. During his New York days in the comics business, he did some outlines for an authorized Saint comic strip, and Charteris liked them enough to want full scripts—liked them so much, indeed, that he had a ghost writer work three of them up as novels. The strip was in time killed because the stories went on at novelistic length, far beyond the attention span of the typical comics reader. At a meeting with Charteris, Harrison was asked if he would care to ghost a novel from one of the scripts he had previously submitted. Harrison leaped at the chance, having just gone free-lance a few years earlier, and hungry for any job of writing.

So while in Denmark he turned out *Vendetta*, after making a study of the Charteris clichés, his creaky style of rhodomontade and failed humor, not to say a studied analysis of the Saint himself, one of those English gentlemen heroes who crush villainy as a hobby, and with a sense of invincibility reaching to smugness. Yet the Saint proved to be a popular and highly profitable character second only to Sherlock Holmes. Harrison's problem, he said, "was to write the thing without making it a parody." He somehow resisted the temptation and wrote a clever story set in Sicily (where the Saint had never been before), the only mafia novel to my knowledge that sets forth the historical origins of that word as an acronym for the Italian resistance movement during the period of French rule over the Two Sicilies. M-A-F-I-A is a thirteenth-century slogan, *"Morte alla Francia, Italia anela"* (Italy wishes death to France!) (book 2, chapter 4). Charteris did not change a word in the manuscript and on publication signed the book with the words, " 'But for whom . . . etc.'—& for once that old cliché is true!" Well, more than once.[1]

Black Thriller

The above term is Harrison's for the international suspense novel. His one work in this genre is *The QE2 Is Missing* (1980). The book was prompted by the suggestion of an English publisher of paperback originals designed and promoted to be best-sellers. The idea thrown out was to do something up-to-date with the idea of a mysteriously abandoned ship, harking back to the famous case of the *Mary Celeste*. Harrison picked up on that idea and added, "Why not Queen Elizabeth the Second?" So he signed on and did the book, but two weeks before it was due to come out the publisher went bankrupt. "No sales program, no best seller—I was doomed by the stupid vagaries of publishing," Harrison says ruefully.

The book itself, however, is a brilliant one for its kind and deserved more success. Its mix of ingredients alone is the stuff from which best-sellers are made, starting with the *Queen Elizabeth II*, "mightiest liner ever built," missing on a Pacific cruise, with the ships and airplanes of more than twenty nations unable to find her. On board are all the major characters in the story. At the center is the archetypical innocent, a Jewish-American lawyer (and his fiancée), pulled into the resolution of a story problem entailing an Israeli Nazi-hunter sworn to capture the German paymaster of Nazis exiled in Paraguay, who carries $250,000,000.00 in diamonds to buy arms for General Alfred Stroesser, "life-time president" of Paraguay (now deposed) and dependent on Nazi help (as they need his protective regime) to stem the tide of revolution from the Tupamaro guerrillas. Also on board is a terrorist team of these very same revolutionaries, whose aim is to seize the documents pertaining to this arms deal and publicize them, so as to arouse popular revolt at home and loathing abroad—and to do so in a most dramatic way. Hence the disappearance of the QE2, meant to be found (as she is in time), but empty of crew and passengers for added publicity, and finding *them* (given Harrison's intelligent use of exotic geography) is not so easy.

Techno-Thriller

This heading is taken from the title of a *New York Times* article about Tom Clancy entitled "King of the 'Techno-Thriller.' " Clancy had been a best-selling author from the start of his career with *The Hunt for Red October* (1984), followed by huger successes with novels like *Red Storm Rising* (1986) and *The Cardinal of the Kremlin* (1988). Apart from their suspenseful plots, his books have much in common with technophilic science fiction, given Clancy's extensive display of technical knowledge—in his case the technology of submarines, missiles, computers, satellites, lasers, and every sort of military hardware. This all seems to appeal to the public, despite the difficulty Clancy had in finding his first publisher; the others thought it, well, too technical. Above and beyond that, however, is another matter mentioned by the *Times* journalist who interviewed him. "Perhaps the key factor in Clancy's phenomenal success in his unabashed patriotism. His novels center on the United States-Soviet rivalry, and his view is simple: 'I think we're the good guys and they're the bad guys. Don't you?' "[2]

Harrison's techno-thriller, *Skyfall* (1976), is a rhetorical match in every respect except the latter. It is the story of a joint United States-Soviet mission in space, its mixed crew united in the conquest of nature on behalf of mankind. Six men and women, American and Russian, are launched into orbit in the 2000-ton Prometheus, the largest spacecraft ever built, on a mission to place in stationary orbit a mighty solar generator for the beaming of power to an energy-depleted world of the near future. Hence the name Prometheus, the Titan in Greek mythology who stole fire from the gods and gave it as a gift to mankind. Its cabin and instruments are American-made; its rockets' engines are Lenin-5 boosters, five fission engines fueled by uranium 235.

Once in orbit, one of its engines, damaged in takeoff, will not start again; because all five are interconnected, unlike chemical engines, many hours will be needed to cut the malfunctioning one out of the system. But there is no time for this, because an unpredictable solar flare has erupted on the rim of the Sun, revolving towards the face of the Earth, where its effect will be felt in the heat expansion of the atmosphere. The Prometheus, in low orbit, is fated to brush against its upper fringes as it swells outwardly; a solid wall of air, in effect, is what the Prometheus is going to run into, since it now cannot boost itself into higher orbit. The ship will fall to Earth with 500 pounds of radioactive uranium pellets aboard, spewing deadly atomic gasses into global circulation as it makes its fiery plunge through the atmosphere, causing a disaster for all humanity. The astrophysics of this crisis, and all other scientific and technical details, is perfectly realized with the most convincing specificity.

The crew members seem to be doomed, since the relief shuttle is a month away from launch, and it will take days to ready it ahead of schedule. Contemplating their fate, not to say that of all mankind, one of the Americans (not a combat pilot like the original spacemen) is given to share with the Russians the obligatory sentiment: well, so much for "all our little nationalism and fears" (chapter 35). Meanwhile, back on Earth, those fears are raised to a new pitch. As one of the book's promotional ads puts it, "The lethal radioactive fuel, Uranium 235, which the vessel is carrying, gives the crisis an acute international urgency, and the politicians play out their power games in the light of this desperate knowledge."[3]

The Russian politicians, given even-handed treatment with the wicked Americans, but not quite as wickedly even-handed, unilaterally decide to blow up the Prometheus while it is still in orbit by shooting a missile at it; but the missile misses. The reactionary, liberal-bashing, hack of a politician who is the president of the United States refuses advice to launch a rescue mission (one of the crew members is by now badly injured by the missile blast), using a space shuttle already on the launching pad, ready to put a secret CIA device in orbit, a powerful laser able to zap the Kremlin from outer space. But no; the militarization of space, in defiance of the other side's peaceful uses of space, comes first. (Surely it is disingenuous to suggest that secret CIA payloads lofted by the American shuttle fleet are anything other than spy satellites for the peaceful monitoring of arms agreements, troop readiness, and the like; or that any U.S. president of Ronald Reagan's conservative stripe, as in the novel, would authorize the CIA to usurp the Defense Department's procurement and deployment of strategic weapons systems.) But everything is eventually resolved, presumably to the readers' satisfaction.

Coffee-Table Books

These are handsome, oversized, illustrated works of nonfiction. *Great Balls of Fire!* (1977) reveals all in its subtitle, "A History of Sex in Science Fiction Illustration." Actually, sex merely serves as a foil; Harrison's informed text is rather more a history of the genre, told with his characteristic wit and verve. The book contains hundreds of pictorial examples drawn from a vast variety of sources; recent and very sophisticated European and American artists are highlighted.

Mechanismo (1978) contains less text relative to illustration—the work of nineteen contemporary artists whose paintings are displayed in color in full- or double-page spreads. The pictures provide the excuse for Harrison's brief historical chapters on "Starships," "Mechanical Man," "Weapons and Space Gear," "Space Cities," and "Fantastic Machines," with a final chapter on "Movies."

Most interesting is *Planet Story* (1979), done in collaboration with the artist Jim Burns, whose lavishly displayed paintings Harrison commissioned for his book. The interest here is that he wrote the story as a device for the artist to fully exercise his talents. Usually the illustrator comes in after the book is written, and he has little variety to play with, given the writer's own concern with the story's linear plotting. But here, Harrison contrived a plot with the artist first in mind, giving him something new and interesting to illustrate in every chapter.

Spacecraft of Fact and Fiction (1979), done in collaboration with the editor Malcolm Edwards, is exactly what the title indicates. It surveys the idea of spacecraft from the earliest imaginings, and as realized in modern achievement. The illustrations range from pictures of historical fantasies through to the moon landing and the space shuttle, and on to imaginings of interstellar travel in the far future.

Juveniles

Books for juveniles are a good source for steady earnings, and Harrison has done very well in having his three titles in this field recommended by school librarians, who are responsible for the bulk of the sales. *Spaceship Medic* (1970) is a technophilically detailed tale about a young paramedic who learns to assume personal responsibility. *The California Iceberg* (1975) narrates how young Todd Wells (based on Harry's own son Todd) learns about drought relief and aids the effort. *The Men from P. I. G. and R. O. B. O. T.* (1978) is a jollier tale about a herd of specially trained pigs that help a Space

Patrol officer bring law and order in the distant future to Earth's colonies on planets far away, followed by one about sentient robots that serve in the same way. Possibly Harrison's greatest success so far, however, has been with a series of books that have proved especially popular with young readers, but that also have won a far wider audience throughout the world. These books are the subject of the next chapter.

Chapter Nine
Thief as Hero

At Windycon 13 held in Chicago in 1987, Harrison autographed 5000 books, "of which 4,999 were 'Rat' books," he says with only slight exaggeration. These *are* his most popular titles (especially among juveniles); he estimates that "about 90 percent of new books signed are 'Rat' books." Incidentally (or not so incidentally, if a sidelight on celebrity is appreciated), he says that at autographing sessions his accomplished method allows him to sign 1000 copies per hour.

The first book in the series was *The Stainless Steel Rat* (1961), developed around a character, James Bolivar diGriz ("Slippery Jim"), who appeared in the first two short stories Harrison placed in ASF (1957 and 1960; see chapter 2), but who had not yet acquired the sobriquet given him in the book title. Then followed *The Stainless Steel Rat's Revenge* (1970), another rather serious "world saving" story. With *The Stainless Steel Rat Saves the World* (1972) and *The Stainless Steel Rat Wants You* (1979), in which diGriz does his humanity-saving bit disguised as a hideous alien from the enemy stars, the series evolved into madcap entertainment at the expense of serious message-sending— although the Harrison message remained implicit, quietly understated in Slippery Jim's ethical code whatever his fool adventures.

At that point, after three or four titles, Harrison began to notice their popularity. This is partly due to the fact that they got funnier as he went along; and perhaps they really did grow in popularity. The first and second titles were not as funny as they could have been, because, as Harrison says, he had to sell them as straight adventure stories and "sneak in the humor." The trouble is, "You must have a reputation as a humorist to publish humor; it's a difficult market to break into, as each editor has his own idea of humor, unlike his perception, say, of a Western. So I built up the proportion of lightness in each 'Rat' book until there was more humor than adventure; and now it's the humor that's advertised. Now I'm a 'humorist.' "

Despite editors' misgivings, Harrison's comic sensibility came across from the start, and readers asked for more. He was only too happy to oblige, since doing a light weight book between serious books was a relief from the latter's heavy research costs, both in time and effort; he writes a "Rat" book in about a year.

The opening paragraphs from the initial title will convey something of Slippery Jim's attitude toward his chosen profession. By the way, the first three paragraphs comprise the storyless "narrative hook" of a long-ago exercise that awakened Harrison's curiosity and stimulated him to play it out (see chapter 2):

When the office door opened suddenly I knew the game was up. It had been a money-maker—but it was all over. As the cop walked in I sat back in the chair and put on a happy grin. He had the same somber expression and heavy foot that they all have—and the same lack of humor. I almost knew to the word what he was going to say before he uttered a syllable.

"James Bolivar diGriz I arrest you on the charge—"

I was waiting for the word *charge*, I thought it made a nice touch that way. As he said it I pressed the button that set off the charge of black powder in the ceiling, the crossbeam buckled and the three-ton safe dropped through right on the top of the cop's head. He squashed very nicely, thank you. The cloud of plaster dust settled and all I could see of him was one hand, slightly crumpled. It twitched a bit and the index finger pointed at me accusingly. His voice was a little muffled by the safe and sounded a bit annoyed. In fact he repeated himself a bit.

" . . . On the charge of illegal entry, theft, forgery—"

He ran on like that for quite a while, it was an impressive list but I had heard it all before. I didn't let it interfere with my stuffing all the money from the desk drawers into my suitcase. The list ended with a new charge and I would swear on a stack of thousand credit notes *that* high that there was a hurt tone in his voice.

"In addition the charge of asaulting a police robot will be added to your record. This was foolish since my brain and larynx are armored and in my midsection—"

And *that* is what Harrison calls "disguised humor." What it is like undisguised in the later titles, the reader can discover only by reading them. They really are not as "juvenile" as their targeted audience might indicate. The adult reader can find much amusement in them at a more sophisticated level of appreciation.

Slippery Jim's profession is that of master criminal, operating in the thirtieth century, when a galactic empire of worlds is policed so well that crime is almost unknown—certainly the kind of stupendous con jobs that diGriz pulls off are rare indeed. Only one other man has achieved a reputation for that kind of professional work, the Bishop, whose example it was Jim's ambition from boyhood to emulate. But, Slippery Jim, the only free-lance pirate in the galaxy, turns legal in the very first title, enlisting with the Special Corps as an interstellar agent in the cause of universal justice, aided by his mastery of crime technique and, in subsequent titles, by help from his like-minded bride, Angelina. (She is wooed in that first title, and remains a faithful partner to the monogamous Jim thereafter.)

The basic model for Jim's adventures is the picaresque novel as perfected by Tobias Smollet (1721–71). Beyond that, Harrison says, the problem was to find a sobriquet fitting the part of "an outsider in a society of the future. As we have flesh and blood rats in wooden buildings, in future—steel rats?" So he reports his thinking, leading on to "the stainless steel rat," which is detailed elsewhere.[1]

This is brought out in one of the later titles, *A Stainless Steel Rat Is Born* (1985), which traces the origins of James diGriz from petty to cosmic criminal, as he seeks out and finds his exemplar, the Bishop, from whom he learns how to improve himself. This archcriminal explains to the young Jim,

"We must be as stealthy as rats in the wainscoting of their society. It was easier in the old days, of course, and society had more rats when the rules were looser, just as old wooden buildings have more rats than concrete buildings. But there are rats in the building now as well. Now that society is all ferroconcrete and stainless steel there are fewer gaps in the joints. It takes a very smart rat indeed to find these openings. Only a stainless steel rat can be at home in this environment."

But the real lesson is that "we" are not to think of ourselves as criminals, but as heroes, "living by a stricter moral code." The Bishop, leading up to the rat business, had said,

"We are Citizens of the Outside. We have rejected the simplistic, boring, regimented, bureaucratic, moral, and ethical scriptures by which they live. In their place we have substituted our own far superior ones. We may physically move among them—but we are not of them. Where they are lazy, we are industrious. Where they are immoral, we are moral. Where they are liars, we are the Truth. We are probably the greatest power for good to the society that we have discarded. (chapter 14)

Yes, the stainless steel rat is a benefactor to society, not in the least by giving the police something to do with their expensive machines and by providing the public with entertaining news about the chase.

As it happens, however, it is the Bishop in his retirement from Outside Citizenship who snags his former pupil in the first "Rat" book, recruiting Jim into the Special Corps of his own making and direction. Jim's turnabout brings into focus the idea behind this chapter's title, "Thief as Hero." It has a long history in life and literature, the latter borrowing from the former. Thanks to Paul Tomlinson's fanzine for the Harry Harrison Appreciation Society, that history was laid out in the 1986 issue; I draw upon it for the following remarks.[2]

Stories about thieves began their popularity in England and France from the late nineteenth century, with their conventional format modeled after the exploits of a real thief famous at that time, Eugene Francoise Vidocq (1775–1857). His life of colorful crimes began in his early teens, but he eventually crossed over into law enforcement and become chef de la sûreté with a staff of twenty-eight, all ex-cons. Vidocq later went into private detective work, occasionally aiding the police, and developed his reputation as a master of disguise. The first detective to employ such methods, he is the obvious original for Sherlock Holmes and all the other fictional masters of the same business. And certainly Edgar Allan Poe was inspired by Vidocq for his amateur detective, Chevallier Auguste Dupin, who figures in his "Murders in the Rue Morgue" (1841).

The romantic qualities of the criminal were played up in four novels written by Edward Bulwer-Lytton (better known for his historical novels, especially *The Last Days of Pompeii*), notably *Paul Clifford* (1830) with its "gentleman highwayman" as hero. Then there is A. O. Raffles, the inverted Sherlock Holmes created by E. W. Hornung (with Bunny playing a crooked Watson), who at career's end turns to the side of the law to play detective in *Raffles, the Amateur Cracksman* (1899). The French Arsine Lupin is a roguish leader of a gang of thieves created by Ponson du Terrail in 1905, a master of disguise (even posing as chef de la sûreté for four years) who finally puts this talent to work in true detective work. Arsine Lupin, however, is but a replay of Terrail's earlier rogue of the Paris underworld, Rocambole, who, after many serialized adventures from 1853, turns detective so as to apply his criminal skills to fighting wrongdoers; yet his wicked habits from the past thrive in the great joy he finds when scoring over the police.

All of these thief-heroes may be seen as ancestors of Slippery Jim. But there is one more of special interest, the outstanding criminal Vautrin created by Honoré de Balzac (1799–1850), who in one story speaks for himself in these words; "In every million men there are ten who put themselves above everything, even the law, and I am one of them." This statement has an exact parallel in the words of diGriz in *The Stainless Steel Rat*. Referring to the petty larceny at large, he says, "That is almost the full extent of crime in our organized, dandified society. Ninety-nine per cent of it, let's say. It is that last and vital one per cent that keeps the police department in business.

That one per cent is me, and a handful of men scattered around the galaxy"
(chapter 2).

The "Rat" books do contain some message content. Jim never carries a gun
and never kills anybody. He is against violence, and is a professed pacifist. In
the latest title, *The Stainless Steel Rat Gets Drafted* (1987), this antimilitary
theme is the principal one. Harrison sent me a fan letter from a reader in the
U.S. Army (a technical sergeant), who thinks it "the best 'Rat' story in the
entire series. Your portrayal of enlisted attitudes (or at least their perception)
about the Army is accurate, even with today's Volunteer Army."

The story starts with Jim chasing down the traitor who had caused the
death of his friend and mentor, the Bishop. The trail leads to the invincible
land of Nevenkebla, where, under a different identity, this fiend is discovered
to be General Zenna—crazed head of a gathering army bent on conquest of
the planet Chojecki, in violation of peace treaties binding every member of
the Galactic League. Posing as a local youth of eighteen (he is nineteen), Jim
is drafted into this army, as is every Nevenkeblan youth. His induction into
the ranks is treated with Harrison's usual barbed-wire humor for things military. The troops are issued Yuk-E rations in a plastic container that, a moment after being filled for a quick drink of water, shrinks and softens to
become a government issued contraceptive.

In due time, the rockets blast into space as General Zenner's unbeatable
army is launched against the unarmed and defenseless Chojecki. But this
army has been penetrated by the Rat. The odds of success are three million
soldiers to one Stainless Steel Rat. Can he alone, single-handedly, pit himself
against the most destructive army in the known universe? You bet he can!

When the army invades Chojecki, it finds that the planet has no armies or
police. But the army wants a war anyway. "Medals don't go to generals who
bring back the troops intact," says General Zenner. "Battle! That's where the
glory is! There will be fighting, mark my words. It is human nature. They
can't all be cowards on this planet" (chapter 16).

What Chojecki has, instead of military defenses, is an unbeatable philosophy, Individual Mutualism. And this is what the Rat has working for him
when, in the book's highest point of delirious comedy, the invading army
breaks up when confronted by Individual Mutualism, not at all the cowardly
thing General Zenner thinks it is. Not a single reviewer, however, has picked
up on what it really is, a hard-nosed anarchism, despite the giveaway in the
use of famous anarchist names like that of Czolgoscz.

But above all, the message of the Rat is in the language "he speaks like a
native" (as Harrison says): Esperanto. In response to readers asking about Esperanto, the author placed an answer at the back of *The Stainless Steel Rat for*

President (1982). (Here Jim, still with the Special Corps, liberates a backward planet from the clutches of an aging dictator of the Latin American type—by rigging the elections his own way.) The back of the British edition contains information on how to contact the British Esperanto Centre; the American edition explains how to reach a like center in this country. Harrison's closing words in each case are, "The Stainless Steel Rat's advice—and mine as well—is to write a postcard to the following address: [address given]. It will change your life!"

Esperanto is a durable, but still not universal, artificial language which celebrated its one hundredth birthday in July 1987. It is the creation of Dr. L. L. Zamenhof, a Polish eye doctor of Jewish heritage who grew up in nineteenth-century Belostock, Russia—now Bialystok, Poland—where he witnessed constant quarreling among Russians, Poles, and immigrant German textile workers. He decided that if people spoke a common language their tiresome differences would vanish. So he constructed a new language to replace national languages. Fearful, however, that his unconventional idea would drive away patients, he published it under a pen name, Doctor Esperanto, or, "the one who hopes."

Within the last two generations there have been many attempts to aid international communication by the invention of other artificial languages to the same purpose, to foster international amity and prevent wars. Examples are Volapük, Ido, Antido, Novial, Solresol, Interglossa, Ro, and Mongling. But only Esperanto has grown into a fully fledged language with its own international speech community of perhaps two million fluent speakers (eight million altogether counting those less fluent).[3]

Indeed, Harrison has written a science fiction story in Esperanto and published it in an Esperanto literary magazine.[4] Esperanto is, after all, a sort of science fiction idea. H. G. Wells, in *The First Men in the Moon* (1901), pronounced upon the failings of mankind, "still not united in one brotherhood," when he reported the viewpoint of the dictator of a world socialist state existing in the moon: "The Grand Lunar was greatly impressed by the folly of men clinging to diverse tongues. They want to communicate and yet not communicate" (chapter 24).

But Harrison's interest goes beyond the science fictional. In 1986 he attended the 71st annual international congress of the Universala Esperanto Asocio, held in Beijing, the largest international cultural meeting ever hosted by China. To express his own good will at that event, he distributed to the Chinese delegates a credit card–sized computer run by light or sunlight, custom-inscribed on the back with the legend: "Esperanto / 1986 / Pekino." More, Harrison attended as no mere member but as a patron. This distinction he earned in 1981, when the association's world body named him as one of its eight honorary patrons, consisting of linguists, scientists, and other eminent people who have made "grave services" to the Esperanto movement, and who themselves speak and write the international language (see all recent editions of the *Esperanto Yearbook*). Among those on the Honora Patrona Komitato is the president of the Swedish parliament; Harrison asked me to mention that "he is the only person in Sweden who can fire any member of the Swedish Parliament—and the king!"

Earlier, the Esperanto Association of Ireland had named Harrison its honorary president. It all began, however, with his boredom with army life. Attending a lecture on the subject, looking for anything to keep his mind alive, he got a little book from the speaker, *Learn Esperanto in 17 Easy Lessons*. He then learned to read and write Esperanto and used it for correspondence, but never heard it spoken. When he went to New York after the war and heard people speaking it for the first time, "I couldn't follow them at all. So I went to class and after a few weeks learned to speak as well as read and write it, and I've never looked back since."[5]

But there is one more "Rat" title to deal with, of a type known as the interactive game book, *You Can Be the Stainless Steel Rat* (1985). It is chopped up into 343 disconnected paragraphs numbered as such, with "The End" coming after number 338. Addressed to the reader as a new recruit to the Special Corps, the Rat himself gives the orders, and puts the recruit onto his first assignment. Most crucial to this type of book, the Rat can advise only on the alternatives to be taken in any new situation: turn to number this or number that (up to four choices), which prove to be a smart move or a stupid one, according to the reader's decision. As I tried to follow out all the alternatives at once, I soon got lost in an ever-branching tree. How Harrison controlled the writing of this prolix tangle completely baffles me. But for the role-playing recruit who reads it in the intended spirit, it must be quite an absorbing—not to say amusing—experience.

The role enjoyed by the reader in this game is that of "thief as hero." Nobody forces him into this life of crime; it is fun. Never mind that he follows advice from a Rat now working for the Special Corps; the special kicks to be gotten from a self-consciously deviant style of behavior are the same, be they criminal techniques belonging to Citizens of the Outside or to regular citizens working in a highly irregular manner for the law. What then of nonheroic thieves? Harrison keeps insisting that he disbelieves in "the Catholic devil theory of evil"; instead he believes that crime is a product of social forces, mainly of poverty created by a selfish and uncaring society. The model for this rather widespread and enduring version of amateur criminology is hungry Jean Valjean stealing a loaf of bread in *Les Misérables* (1862) by Victor-Marie Hugo.

Now comes a sociologist from the University of California at Los Angeles to examine this assumption, long dismissed by common sense: bakeries in our society are not conspicuously besieged. Professor Jack Katz, in *Seductions of Crime* (1988), argues that most crime is motivated neither by greed nor need, but by the "sneaky thrills" that come with violating the law as an end in itself. The common motive is to create "a morally unacceptable self" and maintain it with a sense of righteousness against social authority. Killers apart (for whom another kind of righteousness applies), shoplifters and burglars and muggers really are little devils, after all.[6] And so is the Rat and his recruits.

Chapter Ten
Adventures Past, Present, and Future

Harrison's dictum that science fiction is not limited to storytelling about the future is here put to the test, with stories about both past and present. This generous view of the genre is not held by everybody in the trade. For example, Frank Herbert had trouble placing *The Santaroga Barrier* (1968) in the magazines, until Harrison bought it for *Amazing* during his pinch-hitting tenure there, because it was not viewed as being science fiction, for it is set in the present with a most commonplace-looking background. What makes it science fiction?

The little Californian town of Santaroga is unusual for the exotic drug its inhabitants take under the eye of a resident psychologist, who has a remarkable theory about its possible social effects on the outcome of human civilization. The town's apartness from the outside is the "barrier" the narrator is given to cross and explain, filling in for the reader the seemingly normal but, under close inspection, the strangely different conditions of Santarogan culture; this he does as he would in reporting the novelties of any future society.[1] The rule in science fiction is, first develop the unfamiliar background, then develop character (in practice, this is done concomitantly).[2]

Similarly with science fiction set in the past. But how do such stories differ from historical novels?

Past

Stonehenge (1972) is a novel Harrison and I wrote together, and we discussed this question from the start. We determined that we were not writing a historical novel but a novel *about* history, whose purpose was to authenticate the past. Historical novelists do not as a rule aim at this. Rather, they take psychologically modern people with more or less modern problems and project them against a painted backdrop of historical detail researched from secondary sources; rarely if ever does an original theory guide the use of such sources. But in *Stonehenge*, the "proto-Celtic" culture

of the ancient Britons (a concept later established in the technical literature[3]) is not used as ornamental detail but is a key element in our reconstruction of a warrior society in the condition described by Homer and the
sagas of the Irish Celts. It was an effort to dramatize a realistic solution to
the Stonehenge mystery in light of archaeology, classical accounts of the
Gaulish Celts, and Indo-European epic literature.

When the novel first was published, the dagger carving on the inner face
of stone no. 53 was believed to have represented a royal Mycenaean dagger,
indicating a Mediterranean connection dating back to 1500 B.C. That connection is dramatized in the person of Ason, the novel's hero. But since then, a
revision of the radiocarbon chronology has pushed the date of the final phase
of Stonehenge back to 2000 B.C., which is about 500 years *before* the rise of
Mycenae. Therefore the dagger carving is later than the monument, whose
construction was a strictly local accomplishment.

All the same, my political interpretation of the monument (in contrast to
the astronomical interpretation) is not shaken. I still hold to its function as a
royal election court for the elevation of Bronze Age kings or chieftains, long
before royalty passed from elective to dynastic status. In *Stonehenge: The Indo-European Heritage* (1979), I argue this theory on scholarly grounds, having playfully tested the idea in a novel beforehand, with Harrison's
wonderful adventure story to give it life. The matter of the revised chronology, assumed for this other book, is related in the afterword of a later, full-
length edition of the novel, retitled as *Stonehenge: Where Atlantis Died*
(1983). That title may seem out of place for a serious novel about history (or
prehistory), but it is defended in the afterword, to which a pertinent bibliography is attached.

One other feature, perhaps the most important one, marks this novel as
science fiction: its backplotting. The last lines, concerning how the dagger
carving got on stone on stone no. 53, were written first. Everything else was
plotted toward that revelation, by way of accommodating both background
as foreground and theory as hero. It is not a novel of character, as regular historical novels are; it is, and can be, nothing else but science fiction.

Present

Plague from Space (1965) might remind the reader of Michael Crichton's
The Andromeda Strain (1969). Harrison says the reminder ought to be the
other way around; except that the latter was made into such a big "sci-fi"

thriller of a film in 1971[4] ("sci-fi" being his term of contempt), all memory traces of the real connection have been obliterated.

Harrison's aim was to write a novel of "decent medical SF, tapping a reservoir of knowledge from the medical journalism." The journalistic allusion points to the year he spent while in Denmark researching and writing for the *Medical Tribune* (see chapter 2). As nothing of the kind had yet been done, he decided to fill the gap with a story built around the real science of medicine as it is known today, instead of the fantasy medicine so typical of futuristic science fiction.

The story problem is put in motion with the return of a manned space mission to Titan, one of the satellites of Saturn. This places the time as a near future, by now even nearer, since the *New York Times* for 29 November 1988 reports a NASA plan to launch a probe toward Titan, land it on the surface, and there collect soil samples for possible evidence of life. Even so, the setting of the medical problem is all but contemporary, which justifies classifying the novel here in the "present." After all, Michael Crichton saw *Plague from Space* as a source from which to borrow for his present-day medical drama, or at least Harrison's editor at Doubleday so suspected.

The mission's commander returns alone, riddled with a horrible—and unknown—fatal disease. The ship is immediately sealed and quarantined, but not soon enough. The disease spreads, killing hundreds and sparing none from fear. Working against the pressures of time and mass hysteria, a medical team, consisting of a doctor and his attractive partner, a superb pathologist, tries to find a cure for the raging disease. But there is no love interest here; professional comradeship, not love, binds the doctor and the pathologist. The real narrative subject of the story is epidemiology (the question of disease vectors and related matters), as only the science fiction mode of storytelling can relate it; and the resolution of the problem is realistic and plausible.

The Daleth Effect (1970), set in contemporary time, is the American publisher's title (followed by the British) for the author's original, "In Our Hands, the Stars," as it appeared serially in ASF (December 1969; January, February 1970). Here I must note that a regular feature of ASF is its editorial pages; when John W. Campbell was writing them, they covered all manner of topics, at times in an opinionated and political manner, but often with expert insights into questions of science and engineering. It is from these editorials that Harrison in 1966 drew the substance for *Collected Editorials from Analog.*

As Harrison tells of the genesis of *Daleth*, he was thinking a "what if" question: "Suppose a big invention by a small country." At the same time, he was reading a Campbell editorial on the surprising practical effects of a rocket supplied with enough power to run continually (doing more than just boost itself into space and coast as is the case with present limitations): "Accelerating and then decelerating at one G all the time, it gets to the moon in no less than five hours, to Mars in about a day and a half. Only the power supply is the problem." Harrison then went to Campbell and asked, "Where do we get this limitless power supply from?" Campbell suggested speculating on some possible flaw in Newton's Law of Gravitation that serious research might uncover.

So there was the story, ready to write itself. An Israeli physicist, Professor Arnie Klein, doing gravity research at the University of Tel-Aviv, stumbles across just such a flaw with explosive results, blowing out a portion of his laboratory and attracting the interest of his government's military R & D establishment. But Arnie knows better than anyone what he is on to: a power so limitless as to make possible a peaceful world, ending once and for all the wars of imperialism to control scarce energy resources. The expression "Daleth Effect" comes from the Hebrew letter *daleth* or D that Klein assigned as a symbol to the discrepancy factor in Newtonian law that he discovered.

Arnie escapes the security guard placed around him and flees to Denmark. The government of this peaceful little country understands his big purpose and sets him up with facilities for applied research. A power unit making use of the Daleth Effect is installed in a research vessel of the Danish navy, the MS *Vitus Bering*, its only submarine, which is devoted solely to the good purpose of marine biology. Sealed and air-supplied for underwater work, it will serve just as well as a spaceship. Indeed, Arnie is aboard her manning the engines when she is secretly flown to the moon (in less than five hours), where the Danish government reaps its reward by setting up an industrial laboratory for the processing of materials that is possible and profitable to undertake only in a complete vacuum (as in outer space).

The Daleth Effect is revealed to the world when Arnie employs the sub to rescue a Soviet cosmonaut, stranded in orbit in *Vostok 4*. Then the two great powers close in, ruthlessly, to steal the secret. But there is no secret, because Nature keeps no secrets. Science is international, and once the Daleth Effect is known to exist, the secret becomes an open book to all physicists who now know what to look for. The discrepancy factor, once it has been uncovered and utilized, is for all to understand and use practically, as the Japanese are the first to do in developing inexpensive energy packs for all forms of transportation and power generation.

Arnie is killed in the struggle between the superpowers. But his Danish friends meditate that perhaps the politicians will learn a lesson from his death: his discovery was meant "for the mutual good of all mankind" and not for "turning it into one more fantastically destructive weapon." Looked at this way, his death is not a waste. "And so we now all live in the same suburbs of the same world city. That fact will take some getting used to" (chapter 25). Hence the cosmic significance of the original title, "In Our Hands, the Stars." The politicians must now get used to the fact that, as Voltaire would have it, we are all citizens of the universe, our nations but suburbs of one world city.

As Denmark itself is very much the hero of this novel, it is worth explaining why. In the words that follow, I speak sociologically, even statistically, and not personally; although my acquaintance with Harrison's Danish friends during my visit to that country is remembered with nothing but friendly pleasure. But it is interesting that Denmark should be symbolic of that already familiar theme of liberation achieved in reaching to the stars.

The two great powers are pictured as equally wicked, with both morally responsible for Arnie's death and morally obtuse concerning his purpose. The one despotic power is equated with the other civic power, even though this latter, the United States, is very much the home of that liberalism of statism and of cultural license that I have remarked upon before. But ah! Denmark—it is more of the same in a little country with no war-making capacity. Like Sweden and Norway, it is one of the most overgoverned nations in the world, in the liberal not the Stalinist sense, with its welfare services paid for out of an income tax that nearly matches income. This is the Scandinavian way to socialism, too "sensible" to socialize production as in the Eastern Block. A provider state, at confiscatory tax rates, acts to replace Divine Providence with material care for everybody from cradle to grave; but with effects on the nation's religious and family life even more striking than in the U.S. Nominally Lutherans, few Danes are churchgoers. Here, the statistics for divorce are one for every two marriages, and the number of children born out of wedlock nearly exceeds that of legitimate ones.[5] Somewhere George Santayana the philosopher wisecracks, "the only thing the modern liberal is interested in liberating is man from his marriage contract." But this is not far from the utopian dream of the young H.G. Wells in 1894, one dreamed all his life: "individualism in ethics, socialism in economy."[6]

Now the question raised by all this is, why is cultural license regarding faith and family taken as a sign of liberty in the face of such costly statism? What is it about Denmark that is being celebrated in *The Daleth Effect?*

Here's the answer as I see it. For the liberal, especially one strongly under the impress of Enlightenment values, the separation of church and state is the paramount condition of freedom. In writing this condition into the U.S. Bill of Rights, the first constitutional recognition that a secular government might preside over and justify a religiously plural society, its framers are rightly said to have set an example for the world's democracies. But it is often wrongly supposed that the framers intended to discourage if not prohibit a civic role for the church, as if the political process itself was to be free of spiritual infusion. Not so. That famous "wall" between church and state was not meant to stand between church and society as well. As it happens, the Bill of Rights was drawn up not in reaction against religion but in reaction against the strong state, a state strong enough, among other things, to establish a single national religion (in the event now established in the name of secular humanism); it was the state power of the European theocracies of feudal vintage that focused attention on the separation of church and state.[7]

By reversing the emphasis it is easy to misplace the liberties of constitutional government, framed as a universal model by Americans of the Enlightenment, and to overlook Denmark's overweening statism, even to uphold it (as do its voting citizens), not alone for the totality of its collateral freedom from religion and other social controls over Wellsian individualism in ethics, but for its being wholly a provider state; since the resulting sacrifice of civic liberty is more than made up for, when the ethical books are balanced, by a spending on social services that is not competitive with defense spending. (As a NATO country, however grudging its membership, it has U.S. protection.) If I am not mistaken, *The Daleth Effect* is of a piece with "The Streets of Ashkelon." The latter's demonstration of emphasis on sufficiency without the Word (religion and instituted morality) is but the flip side of the same coin, whose obverse is intolerance of the church and whose reverse in tolerance of the state.

I would now like to turn to *Invasion Earth* (1982). Harrisons says that he wrote it to meet the need of his publisher Tom Doherty for an illustrated book to place as one of a series in the nonadult market, "pure adventure for juveniles, with lots of pictures, and a little boost for fem lib at the end." But, he adds, his policy is, "Always give the reader more than he expects." The result is a new and original turn on the invasion theme, derived from *The War of the Worlds* (1898) by H. G. Wells. Indeed, Harrison began by asking himself, "What can I do with that old classic?" As the outcome has its main interest in the way it is revealed, or discovered by the story's hero and "fem lib" heroine, I shall be giving away nothing of real substance if in this case I "back plot" my account of it.

Two subspecies of the same species of alien beings are lost or derelict, far from home with only two or three ships; their plan is to stage an "invasion" of Earth as a means of getting the Earthlings to supply them with uranium fuel, under the guise of aiding one alien side against the other. The one side (enemy) is based on the moon, the other (defending) is based at the South Pole, where fake rayguns are installed, requiring U-235 to power them, or so the deception goes. Meanwhile, to make the invasion's cover story more realistic, the aliens blow up some American cities with atomic bombs; only American cities are destroyed, yet this external threat draws the two superpowers together to meet it. The Earth's heroes are a male American army colonel and a female Russian linguist, who discovers that both sides talk the same language. "The Big Lie" is uncovered, and it becomes evident that the alien ship that crashed in Manhattan at the start of the story was the opening sacrifice in this elaborate ruse. The ship's dead crew and burnt-out power system, which can no longer provide any information about the alien technology, is no longer the mystery it once was, when the one surviving passenger, posing as a prisoner of the other side, began telling the lies that set the invasion game in motion. In the end, the colonel leads a raid on the Antarctic base and, capturing the remaining alien ship that is parked there, uses it to strike the lunar base as well. End of fake invasion. The aliens were vulnerable all along, and they failed to conceal that fact.

But humanity benefits as much as it did from Wells's Martians, who died of a terrestrial bacteria following their real invasion of our planet. Wells concludes *The War of the Worlds* with its narrator's observation, "It may be that in the larger design of the universe this invasion from Mars is not without its ultimate benefit for men . . . the gifts to science it has brought are enormous, and it has done much to promote the conception of the commonweal of mankind" (book 2, chapter 10). So, too, at the end of *Invasion: Earth*, when the general in charge of operations has this to say. "The threat is removed, the war is over, we have scientific evaluations of their technology, as well as their ship to examine." But the Russian heroine is unhappy that the general's military services were needed:

"But don't you have any qualms? Doubts? Don't you realize just how wonderful it would have been if we had taken this opportunity, just once in mankind's bloody history, to succeed by peace and not by war?

"To hold out the hand of brotherhood to the galaxy. Not the streaming red hand of death." (chapter 23)

This after the aliens with their playful game had incinerated a dozen American cities? At all events, the advanced science and technology of the aliens are now humanity's, and a genuine "Rescue Operation" (to hark back to that story title) is now in the offing—mankind's global economy will be saved from unequal growth and development. The past is past; but now, prosperity and peace for all, as all become citizens of the universe.

Future

Deathworld (1960) was Harrison's first novel, long in the making as recounted in chapter 2. The setting is Pyrrus, a frontier planet of the far future, on which every form of nonhuman life, both flora and fauna, mutation upon mutation, has undergone a savage evolution and become a deadly weapon directed at the extermination of man. Even the genetically hardened native Pyrrans cower behind the barricades of a fortress city. (They are armed with blasters that leap into the hand, at the mere pointing of a trigger finger, from power holsters fixed to the gun arm, a device Harrison says he derived from his wartime work with power turrets.) Enter Jason dinAlt, a psychic gambler and accomplished rogue, who answers a Pyrran call for help; the vegetation and everything else is getting more murderous the more it is blasted. Maybe he can understand it; he does. The local psychic life has evolved into incredibly deadly forms in defense against the hostile thoughts of the human colonizers. Violence begets violence. Appalled by the conditions, he fights a singlehanded war, not only with the planet, but with its murder-minded people. His difficult message for them is, "We become what we hate."

This phrase, exactly representing the theme of the book, and the specific lesson to be learned from it, is taken from the title of an op-ed piece in the *New York Times* from some years ago. The editorial makes the point that we Americans, animated by hatred of the German people and especially the Japanese, hit by our "racist" atom bombs during the World War II, have become a hateful society; now "we are the largest militarist state in the world. We have become our enemy."[8] This, too, is the Harrison message; for the planet Pyrrus is named after the ruinous victory of King Pyrrhus of Epirus over the Romans near the river Siris, from which derives the proverbial "Pyrrhic victory."

In *Deathworld 2* (1964; originally serialized as "The Ethical Engineer" in ASF, July and August 1963), Jason dinAlt survives being marooned on a planet with viciously competitive cultures, and in *Deathworld 3* (1968; serialized the same year as "The Horse Barbarians" in ASF, February, March, and April), Jason leads the Pyrrans away from their fateful home in the conquest of a rich planet peopled by Mongol-like barbarian warriors (nothing but primitive stupidity here, so the mission is a civilizing one). This latter is a rousing good adventure story, heightened by the careful attention given to the mechanics of a primitive technology where they figure in the plot, but is of little ideological interest.

Not so in the case of *Deathworld 2*. Here is the one Harrison work for which I have discovered the single specimen of previous criticism relating to anything done by him—and that as but a passing commentary in a topical essay on the subject of social science fiction. The essay is by Jerry Pournelle, a fellow science fiction writer and, like myself, the holder of a higher degree in the social sciences. Such a rarity deserves quoting in full:

[Harrison] shows us a hunter-gathering society in which every man's hand is against his neighbor. Those who do not rule are slaves. The masters have neither friends, nor allies, nor faithful dogs, nor watchful robots. Even their women are slaves and are treated as such except for the moments when they share the master's bed. Every member of the band lives only to kill the master and take his place. These small groups spend their lives wandering about a barren land searching for roots. On occasion one master will try to poison another; the motive for the attempt is not clear, but presumably in order to take over his neighbor's slaves.

This is ludicrous. It is obviously unstable: how is it to perpetuate itself? How are children to be born, and who is to care for them? Given that children somehow manage to live, does a master enslave his own sons? What is to prevent what seems the obvious course, one master organizing a clan? Given cooperation and trust, he can arm some of his followers; conquest of his solitary neighbors would follow inevitably. No need to break a butterfly on the wheel; my point is that Harrison, in order to illustrate a political point, has attempted to present what never was and never could be as reality. In another part of his novel he shows us a society of unrestrained and brutal *laissez-faire* capitalism. It is no more believable than his hunter-gatherers. Granted that Harrison hopes to bring us a political message and heap scorn upon advocates of *laissez-faire*; but would not his message have been more effective if he had made his straw men viable?[9]

During our Cornwall interviews, I showed this passage to Harrison, and he responded credibly. For one thing, he said, maybe he allowed only a part of his two societies to be seen. For another, even if all were revealed, maybe he was only making concrete that abstraction contrived by Thomas Hobbes in *Leviathan* (1651), when he speculated on the unsocialized condition of man as being "a condition of war of everyone against everyone."

But what surprises me is that a social scientist should overlook what no social scientist should ever pass over without challenging as a matter of vocational duty. The book argues the case, from the progressive viewpoint of scientific humanism, that traditional morality is different in different times and places; that there is no one morality—no natural law—but a thousand and one moralities. This case is made through Jason dinAlt against a high-handed moral policeman who means to bring him to justice for his past sins (but who succeeds only in marooning the two of them on that planet of Hobbesian warfare). Says Jason, whose vices are virtues where he comes from:

"What you so grandly call—with capital letters and a flourish of trumpets—'Laws of Ethics' aren't laws at all, but are simply chunks of tribal ethos, aboriginal observations made by a gang of desert sheepherders to keep order in a house—or tent. These rules aren't capable of any universal application; even you must see that. Just think of the different planets that you have been on, and the number of weird and wonderful ways people have of reacting to each other—then try to visualize ten rules of conduct that would be applicable in all these societies. An impossible task." (chapter 2)

Not so impossible, despite the distinction Jason draws between ethics as the discipline dealing with right and wrong, and ethos as the moral code belonging to a particular society at a given time in history. Thus Jason asserts that the ten rules of conduct guiding his antagonist—he is thinking of the Ten Commandments—form but the ethos of a particular Old Testament desert tribe, now defunct; they form no part of "any absolute laws of ethics." No such "Universal Laws" exist to be generalized for all human societies at all times. But if ten is a despised number from the standpoint of Bible-bashing cultural relativism, then what about the ten fundamental rules of morality derived by Bernard Gert in his cross-cultural study, *The Moral Rules*?[10] All the basic articles of the Mosaic code have been reinvented over and over again, in like particulars or in subsuming generalities.

To argue otherwise is to confuse natural law with positive law. The former is not to be so easily dismissed, as in "A Criminal Act," in which the gunman on behalf of Zero Population Growth says, it will be recalled, "natural law is man-made and varies with the varieties of religion." Of course it is man-made, to the extent that it is not a product of Nature but of human nature, of man as a culture-producing animal. His moral rules are cultural inventions, to be sure, and culture is learned not inborn. But human nature disposes men to learn some things more easily than others. Natural law expresses in the universal moral rules of mankind its common sense, or what C. S. Lewis calls its "ultimate platitudes of Practical Reason," always joined with religion.[11]

Positive law varies, yes, but always in keeping with these primary platitudes. The story just cited makes much of uncommensurable particularities in positive law, as when the gunman confidently states, "The forms of male and female union are as varied as the societies that harbor them." This is always the favorite example of the cultural relativists, hitting at irrational taboos and the unreasoned prejudice of tradition. Differences about the definition of incest or between polygamy and monogamy come under this head, but these cannot obscure the universals of kinship and marriage and family life. To disavow natural law is to leave society open to its would-be dictators, free to make their own laws above and outside the ordinary human platitudes that everywhere presuppose the idea of freedom. If there is no natural law overarching rulers and ruled alike, then fascism is just as likely the outcome of human destiny as democracy, if not more so.

For all the magnified human differences given play in *Deathworld 2*, it is a relief to turn to *The Lifeship* (1975), written in collaboration with Gordon R. Dickson. The book describes how "a racial oneness with the universe" (chapter 16) is achieved the hard way between humans and the Albernareth, a race of aliens with an all-too-believable religion—once it is understood. At some remotely future date, the human race is divided into aristocratic Adelmen and low-caste arbites. Adelman Giles Steel Ashad finds himself the natural leader of the humans aboard the only lifeship to survive the catastrophic sabotage of their spaceliner's power drive. The lifeship also contains some Albernareth, whose business is the piloting of spaceliners. The story problem concerns survival in the lifeship. It will not be easy! Not only is the lifeship in charge of Albernareth pilots bent on religious suicide, and not only are the Adelman's fellow humans poised to destroy both the aliens (out of racial hatred) and each other (for limited air and food), but hidden among the passengers is the very terrorist who destroyed the spaceliner. For all that, it is a story of muted adventure, moody and reflective.

Less philosophical and more rambunctious is the *To the Stars* trilogy (1981). The blurb on the back of this paperback original promotes it with the following puffery: "Jan Kulozik, a brilliant young electronics engineer on 23rd-century Earth, battles to the stars and back on a desperate and fateful quest. Outcast as a member of a corrupt Earth's privileged elite, banished as a rebel and traitor to a God-forgotten planet, Jan risks his life against unthinkable odds to free the oppressed millions, to sever Earth's tyrannical rule over its far-flung star colonies, and to restore humanity's heritage." The book began what Harrison calls "an inadvertent trilogy." But the book that began the trilogy started very humbly from a very lowly vantage point of observation.

Driving along the California freeways in his midget MG, Harrison took notice for once of the huge trucks rushing past him. From where he sat, he was looking up at the bottoms of the hubcaps of their enormous wheels. Flashing into his mind at that moment was the idea instantly classified and filed away as "wheelworld." Developing it, he wrote a novel about a distant planet with a single road 12,000 miles long, running north and south between two polar areas of seasonal grain production, where this planet's farming population awaits cargo ships from Earth to be loaded with each season's wheat crop—this whole scheme devised as an excuse to display cargo trains rolling on huge wheels instead of on rails. The road itself, carved generations ago from solid rock and mountains leveled by fusion torches, is an object of Jan's interest: "The engineers who had built the Road must have exacted great pleasure from conquering nature in the most dramatic manner possible." His appreciation of this achievement echoes the Saint-Simonian romance of man's unified war on nature replacing warfare among a divided humanity. Accordingly, this outlook raises Jan in his exile to natural leadership of the great wheeled trains that roll on this Road. "I work with machines and am different" (book 2, chapter 15). This in turn echoes a technocratic sentiment of H. G. Wells, who wrote that "machines make men honest" (*The Holy Terror* [1939], book 3, chapter 1, section 16).

One year, however, the ships do not come; and Jan is the only one who knows why (a revolution is brewing back on Earth). Now things are different: the farmers are finally free of their bondage to monocropping, but they resist adapting to the new conditions. As Jan observes, "This is a conservative world and people, for the most part, are troubled by change" (chapter 17). As a promoter of the enlightened view of change and progress, Jan's technophilic honesty gets him into trouble. This is *Wheelworld* (1981), part 2 of the trilogy as it evolved.

It grew to the present size, Harrison explains, because he did so much homework on the background of this one novel, with its revolution offstage, that he had enough material "to get two more novels out of it." They are *Homeworld* (1980; part 1) and *Starworld* (1981; part 3). All of this just because Harrison looked up at those big truck wheels!

Starworld, however, is the most notable of the lot. It details the only realistic space war ever fought in science fiction, the only way it can be fought, "making use of orbital mechanics and firing solid shot." (Once again the sea stories of C. S. Forester proved inspirational.) To that is added a humorous note, actually "a jab at *Star Wars*," Harrison says, in the form of an instructional film entitled, "How Not to Fight a Space War." This bit alone, gratuitously worked into the world-saving story for comic effect, is worth the price of admission.

Chapter Eleven
The Saurolithic Age

By the time the joke in this chapter title is explained, little space will be left to examine the *West of Eden* trilogy (1984–88), Harrison's culminating work. But that little space will be enough. The joke itself explains everything essential.

While visiting Harrison in Denmark to put *Apeman, Spaceman* into final form, we went to the movies one evening to see a trashy monster flick—Danish-made, if I am not mistaken, the title long forgotten. It served up the usual anachronisms about prehistoric reptiles living in the company of human cave dwellers. "Ah," said Harrison, recognizing the pattern once again and now giving it a defining label, "the Saurolithic Age!" To unpack that allusion, step by step, will doubtlessly kill the wit of it but I must make the effort.

Years before, Harrison had heard of my trouble teaching anthropology to students enamoured of the fantasy that prehistoric man lived at the same time as the great prehistoric reptiles. They refused to believe otherwise. And no wonder; the same fantasy is endlessly repeated in the entertainment media. So strong is the public will to believe in this nonsense that, in a story I related to him, it was catered to even in a serious Hollywood film about animal life for which I was interviewed, among other scientists, for some advice—futile as it turned out.

The film was called *The Animal World* (1956), and its makers came to New York City to consult with various experts at the American Museum of Natural History. They talked with people in the insect department, with people in the reptile department, with people in the mammal department, and lastly with people in the people department (anthropology). When the question of prehistoric cavemen came up, I was asked, hopefully, if it was true that dinosaurs and cavemen really did coexist. No, I said; that was a popular misconception. The last of the dinosaurs died out sixty-five million years ago at the end of the Cretaceous period, and the famous European cavemen did not appear until very late in the Pleistocene epoch of the Quaternary period, not more than one hundred thousand years ago. Notes were duly taken—

cavemen and dinosaurs not contemporary; separated by about sixty-five million years.

After the film was produced, we advisors were given a private showing at the museum, everybody nodding with happiness at their sage advice well taken. Until the dinosaur sequence, which was animated. On the screen appeared a weighty brontosaur, half-submerged in shallow waters to help support his ungainly bulk, and properly vegetarian, nibbling some plant food at the edge of his pool. Then the narrator broke in with a stentorian voice to say, "Of course, in the days of the dinosaurs there were no cavemen. But if there had been!!!" On walks Alley Oop alongside the pool, dressed in fur kilts and jauntily bearing a big club, just like in Vincent Hamlin's comic strip, and he is whistling the off-to-work-we-go tune of the Seven Dwarfs. The brontosaur looks up from the sedge with his beady little eyes fixed hungrily on Alley Oop, and then, suddenly carnivorous, arches his great long neck out and over and down to pounce upon this poor innocent worker of the dawn, who is jerked up kicking and screaming in the clutch of mighty jaws and slobberingly chewed to pieces. Then the brontosaur turns again to his weeds, and quiet falls over the forest primeval. They had to get it in there! It was not true—but it just *had* to be, anyhow.

This anecdote impressed upon Harrison all the more forcibly something he already knew: the perseverance in science fiction of the lost world theme. The theme is named after the title of a novel by Conan Doyle, *The Lost World* (1912), in which the intrepid Professor Challenger leads an expedition to a hidden plateau at the upper reaches of the Amazon River where dinosaurs and primitive men still survive. A silent film version from First National, *The Lost World*, appeared in 1925 with special effects by Willis H. O'Brien, who later created the solitary great ape and his prehistoric reptilian companions in *King Kong* for RKO in 1933, remade in 1976 as a big-budget, wide-screen Dino De Laurentiis production. (In both versions, a tribe of Papuan primitives does duty for the usual cavemen.) *The Lost World* has been remade three times: in 1951 as *The Lost Continent*; in 1960 as *The Lost World*; and then in 1968 again as *The Lost Continent*. Closely related is the matching pair, *The Land That Time Forgot* (1975) and *The People That Time Forgot* (1977), based on two same-title stories of 1918 by the American romancer, Edgar Rice Burroughs (1875–1950). The land in question is an island near the South Pole.

Burroughs was an indefatigable miner of this gold-bearing, lost-world lode, which he literally worked subterraneously once he tapped into the hollow-Earth theory of John Cleves Symmes who, in *Symzonia: A Voyage of Discovery* (1820), opened up the planet's interior, via a hole in the South

Pole, to whatever fancy other writers might wish to fill it with. (That is where Poe's hero was headed in his unfinished *Narrative of A. Gordon Pym* [1837].) In his endless "Pellucidar" series, Burroughs filled the Earth's interior with dinosaurs, beastly cave dwellers, and bloodthirsty adventure. He began the series with *At the Earth's Core* (1914, filmed in 1976) and *Pellucidar* (1915), and finished it up with *Back to the Stone Age* (1937), *Savage Pellucidar* (1942), and *Land of Terror* (1944). Even his most famous creation, perhaps the most famous character in the annals of fiction, gets into the act, in *Tarzan at the Earth's Core* (1930). No doubt all of this may be traced to Jules Verne who, in chapter 39 of *Journey to the Center of the Earth* (1864), has his three redoubtable explorers come upon the far shores of an interior sea where they find living fossils in a herd of *Elephas meridionalis* (mastodons) tended by a solitary, antediluvian shepherd of heavy build who stands twelve feet tall—a relic of Neanderthal man, according to the learned professor who leads the party. He recites the record of discovery in French caves of massive jaw bones, in association with hefty stone axes, and reconstructs from them giants, one of whom survives alone in this lost underworld, much as King Kong perpetuates giant apehood all by his lonesome on a lost island in the Pacific. But the trio had already seen enough to prepare them for this when, crossing the sea on a makeshift raft, they are caught in the middle of a fight between a big-jawed plesiosaur with 182 teeth (the professor counts them, checking the number against his reference books) and its ichthyosaurian victim. This occurs in chapter 33 with its archetypical title, "A Battle of Monsters." Elsewhere, they are beset from above by dive-bombing pterodactyls.

Not yet mentioned is the romantic revision of Earth's prehistory as told in films like *One Million B.C.* (1940), starring Victor Mature and Carole Landis, and its remake, *One Million Years B.C.* (1966), starring John Richardson and Raquel Welch—the story of ordinary, working cave people trying to make ends meet in a hazardous environment filled with belching volcanoes, pestiferous pterodactyls, and battling monsters. The prototype for all such stories, on screen or in print, is the enduring, misbegotten little juvenile classic by Stanley Waterloo, *The Story of Ab: A Tale of the Time of the Caveman* (1897). Also influential has been J. H. Rosny the elder's *La felin géant* (1918), translated in 1924 as *Quest of the Dawn Man*.[1]

Alley Oop the stegosaur-riding caveman of the comics is but one mythic expression of the popular longing for an age that never was: the Saurolithic Age. Harry Harrison's preposterous name for this imaginary age derives from *sauro-*, a learned borrowing from the Greek meaning "lizard" and used in the formation of technical terms by zoologists to designate the different species of extinct reptiles (the dinosaurs as a group when loosely considered);

and from -*lithic*, another technical term borrowed from the Greek, this one used in archaeology as an adjectival suffix meaning "of or pertaining to stone." For example, *Paleolithic* means "Old Stone Age." This pertains to the prehistoric cultures of the Pleistocene epoch. It contrasts with *Neolithic*, or "New Stone Age," referring to the farming cultures of the post-Pleistocene or Recent epoch. Paleolithic culture was based on the hunting of large game animals, most, like the mastodon, now extinct. It was during the Paleolithic that the famous cavemen of Europe flourished. But in point of fact their most common habitat was a tent of animal skins; rarely did they live in caves, but even here they pitched their tents, no doubt as double protection against especially hard winters during the cold pulsations of the Ice Age (a vernacular term for the Pleistocene).

The Saurolithic Age, then, is a jocular juxtaposition of the age of the giant reptiles and the Paleolithic or Old Stone Age. When Harrison finally determined on writing *West of Eden*, he said to me, "If it's dinosaurs and caveman they want, then it's dinosaurs and cavemen they're gonna get; only this time the Saurolithic Age will have a rational basis."

Before disclosing his rationale, I must devote some attention to the language of geology and anthropology. Zoologists classify the dinosaurs, but they date their fossils from the geological record. The dinosaurs came and went during the Triassic, Jurassic, and Cretaceous periods of the Mesozoic era, from 225 to 65 million years ago. And while the cultural remains of prehistoric man are the province of the archeologist, these, too, are grounded in the geological record. The first humans appear at the bottom of the Pleistocene epoch of the Quaternary period of the Cenozoic era. All these terms—epoch, period, and era—are from geology. Geologists are not certain when the Pleistocene epoch began—one million years ago? two and a half? three? —but they know when it ended, 10,000 years ago with the end of the Ice Age. The Ice Age as a vernacular term for the Pleistocene is a misnomer, marked as it is by four different ice ages or glacial movements, each named after some feature of geography in the European Alps (Gunz, Mindel, Riss, Würm) or in North America (Nebraskan, Kansan, Illinois, Wisconsin). These glacial episodes are divided by three interglacials and one final retreat of the ice 10,000 years ago, thus heralding the end of the Pleistocene and the beginning of the postglacial or Recent epoch of our own times.

In anthropology, the "lithic" Ages and others of that sort (Bronze Age, Iron Age) are not strictly chronological; while they *do* represent an actual sequence of cultural evolution, they also name types of culture *without* reference to a time frame. For example, the Neolithic or New Stone Age first appears in the archaeological record with the advent of the postglacial epoch.

It is marked by two kinds of evidence: 1) the technological, in particular, tools of composite stone abraded to shape instead of flint hammered or chipped, and 2) economic, the domestication of plants and animals. But Neolithic farming methods (more like gardening than true agriculture) are still the basis of what is called the "underdeveloped" subsistence economy of the world's majority population living in peasant villages; the substitution of iron for stone-tipped hoes and similar changes makes no difference in this taxonomic use of the term. The "primitive stupidity" that Harrison describes in "Rescue Operation" is a judgment on the persistence of the Neolithic way of life in the backwaters of Yugoslavia.

Indeed, not all of the world's people have yet entered even the Neolithic stage of culture; witness, for example, the hunter-gatherer Bushmen of the Kalahari desert. Insofar as they may be viewed as a relic of the Old Stone Age, it is to the tailend of its development, the Epipaleolithic, that they belong. The Paleolithic Age is divided into Lower, Middle, Upper, and Epipaleolithic. This last is also known as Mesolithic (or Middle Stone Age). In the archaeological record, Mesolithic applies to the varied cultures of the skilled hunting peoples who lived between the end of the Würm glaciation and the beginnings of the Neolithic; these peoples are characterized by an elaborate array of finely chipped blade tools (often prepared as blanks for finishing to purpose on the spot), use of the bow and arrow, and domestication of the dog. They are dubbed *skilled* hunters because of their ingenuity in the quest of all sorts of small game and fish, following the decline of large, cold-weather animals, largely killed off by the easygoing rapacity of the Paleolithic hunters before them and brought to final extinction by a tempering of the climate with the onset of the Holocene. (All of the above refers to Old World developments.)

At this point a note on the Eskimo is needed, as an Eskimo-like people, the Paramutan, appears in the *West of Eden* series. Eskimos inhabit the treeless Arctic of North America, the last hunting zone to be occupied by any Mesolithic peoples, probably as late as 1000 B.C., at least 10,000 years after the rest of the continent was filled by the Upper Paleolithic forerunners of today's American Indians. Such a late date is required for the import of a Neolithic technology derived from somewhere on the Asiatic mainland, as the Eskimo use ground-stone knives and adzes to work driftwood for their dog sleds; they also carve lamps out of soapstone or make them of pottery; and they boil their food in kettles of the same materials, using blubber or seal oil as fuel. Stone-grinding, stone-carving, pottery-making, and boiling are all Neolithic techniques.

Eskimo technology has a further complication: the use of oil lamps may be a borrowing from some source of postneolithic civilization. This technique has a long history, going back to the olive-oil lamps of the ancient Middle East, with their undoubted influence on the burning of butter among the Turks and Mongols of Central Asia. The Chinese very early took up the idea in pressing oil from a variety of seeds, and both the Ainu and the Japanese have used fish oil in their lamps. It is possible, however, that the burning of blubber is an independent invention. Anthropologists agree, however, that the Eskimoes could not have adapted a Mesolithic way of life to their environment without drawing upon Neolithic technology, and perhaps also upon one idea suggested by a preexisting civilization.

By civilization is meant a new level of human social organization, one built on the foundations of Neolithic village life and marked by the emergence of urbanism and the political state, as well as by new technologies, principally writing, wheelmaking, and metallurgy. With writing the Historical Age begins, at least in those places where a high culture of priestly or bureaucratic literacy rose above the peasant masses. History first enters the archaeological record in 3500 B.C. with the advent of the Bronze Age in the Middle East (Mesopotamia and Egypt), and with diffusion to other centers of development in the Indus and Yellow River valleys (Harappa and Shang Dynasty China). The New World civilizations (minus wheeled transport) of the Aztecs, Maya, and Incas are difficult to link to Old World precedents in a direct way, but complete cultural autonomy is hardly possible.[2] Nonetheless, the precondition for the rise of civilization is a Neolithic state of culture, itself a recent development coming out of the Paleolithic, by far the longest stretch of human prehistory.

To continue working backward, the Upper Paleolithic was the time of the big-game hunters of the latter half of the Würm glaciation, whose quarry is depicted in the spectacular cave art at Altimira, Lascaux, and other sites in Europe. But these caves are churches not dwellings, and the men who painted them, the Cro-Magnons, are not the model for Ug the Caveman, as in "The Grisly Folk" (1921) by H. G. Wells. Dating from about 35,000 years ago, the Cro-Magnons emerge as modern *Homo sapiens*, man as he is today.

The preceding Middle Paleolithic belongs to Neanderthal Man, living during the Riss-Würm interglacial from about 100,000 years ago and into the Würm glacial. It is the Neanderthals who are the archetypical cavemen, usually portrayed as brutal and stupid, not to say inarticulate, louts; but they were the first humans to bury their dead, indicating some concept of an afterlife—a concept still basic to all the world's religions. Contrary to popular belief, they did not become extinct without issue; nor were they killed out by a superior breed of Cro-Magnon men, as William Golding has it from H. G. Wells in *The Inheritors* (1955). The Neanderthals are in fact the direct ancestors of the Cro-Magnons. Moreover, they were the first to develop a flake-tool technology, evidently mindful of the need to conserve a vanishing resource. Heretofore, in the Lower Paleolithic, core-tools were made from large nodules of flint or quartzite, with most of their mass wasted as discarded flakes. Here belong the hunting cultures of *Homo erectus* and early *Homo sapiens*, both hunters of extinct, big-game animals as were all men of the Old Stone Age. *Homo erectus* is a small-brained ancestor of the entire human lineage, known from both open and cave sites in Europe, the Far East, and Africa. In all these places, the oldest one dating from the bottom of the Pleistocene in South Africa, there is evidence for the domestication of fire— the one crucial technology from which the human revolution itself stems.

Fire provides the open and shut case for determining the human status of *Homo erectus*. This taxon replaces all others (like *Sinanthropus pekininsis* or *Pithecanthropus erectus*) that assign a nonhuman genus to fossil specimens of the erecti. Ancestral to them, in the Pliocene epoch of the Tertiary period, there is nothing human, only the so-called apemen of genus *Australopithecus*. At this point, the story of hominid evolution (*hominid* refers to the whole range of human and prehuman ancestors) is lost in the radial evolution of the nonhuman primates, proliferating in the form of monkeys and apes out of the prosimians of the Paleocene epoch beginning sixty-five million years ago. The ancestral primate, appearing just as the dinosaurs died out, is a small prosimian resembling a tree shrew.

The way is now prepared to understand the rational basis for the Saurolithic Age as Harrison presents it in his *West of Eden* trilogy. Its title is a play on the famous "east of Eden" phrase in Genesis 4:16, thus advising the reader to expect a parallel-world story. And so it is, as the epigraph to volumes 1 and 2 indicates:

The great reptiles were the most successful lifeforms ever to populate the world. For 140 million years they ruled the Earth, filled the sky, swarmed the seas. At this time the mammals, the ancestors of mankind, were only tiny, shrew-like animals that were preyed upon by the larger, faster, more intelligent saurians.

Then, 65 million years ago, this all changed. A meteor six miles in diameter struck the Earth and caused disastrous atmospheric upheavals. Within a brief span of time over seventy-five percent of all the species then existent were wiped out. The age of the dinosaurs was over; the evolution of the mammals that they had suppressed for 100 million years began.

But what if that meteor had not fallen? What would our world be like today?

Harrison had to elaborate on the "today" idea in volume 3, because reviewers without exception had missed it in the other two. So strong was the Saurolithic fancy in its unrationalized form, they all assumed that a story about dinosaurs and Stone Age hunters *must* take place in the prehistoric past and so they duly placed it in 1,000,000 B.C., or whatever Alley Oop's magic date is.

But no; it is a world of *today*, a fictional world with a recorded history like our own, save that its history is in the keeping not of humans but of intelligent dinosaurs. This alternate world came into being because of something that did *not* happen sixty-five million years ago at the end of the Cretaceous period, the fall of an outsize meteor or perhaps an asteroid, whose impact threw up such a darkening dust cloud that it blocked sunlight, halted plant photosynthesis, and starved many species of land animals, including all the dinosaurs. That this *did* happen is a theory proposed in 1980 by Dr. Luis W. Alvarez, winner of the 1968 Nobel Prize in Physics for discoveries in the field of nuclear particles. Most paleontologists, however, disagree; they argue that the decline and extinction of the dinosaurs took a long time and could not have been caused by a single sudden catastrophe. A furious debate heated up the normally staid scientific journals for years, and eventually carried over to popular science magazines, to at last reach general periodicals, and the newspapers.[3] Many of Harrison's readers, then, must be sufficiently aware of this controversy to appreciate the creative use he has made of the Alvarez theory, whatever its merits.

By granting the dinosaurs an extended career of dominance over the Earth, Harrison has allowed for a quite reasonable outcome: the evolution of one intelligent species not unlike man in its capacity for creating culture in the anthropological sense.

This species is his Yilanè, a brainy, erect, bipedal, two-handed dinosaur possessing technology, language, recorded history, state organization, cities, indeed all the attributes of culture and beyond that, of civilization. (Some paleontologists have speculated on one or two late Cretaceous forms as being candidates for possible development analogous to hominid evolution, had there been time for it.) The big difficulty here, as I advised Harrison, was in getting a cultural revolution started for the Yilanè. With humans it began with the mastery of fire, the control over a source of energy external to the body—fire in a way being the "natural" thing for a warm-blooded mammal to master. From that, everything else followed. Next to be controlled was the external nervous energy of the domesticated dog (a good sniffer of game trails) in the Mesolithic, followed by the captured fertility of cultivated plants and barnyard animals in the Neolithic. The whole sequence ends with the burning of fossil fuels for steam power and at last the capture of atomic energy.

But how does a cold-blooded reptile get started in the technology business? I had no answer for Harrison except to say what it could not be: fire. He would have to find some functional equivalent "natural" to cold-bloodedness.

With that puzzler in mind he went to Dr. Jack Cohen, a biologist, and they worked out a brilliant solution. It would spoil the story to tell everything here, but the upshot is that Yilanè technology as it reached its "present-day" powers is driven by the science of genetics. Everything in Yilanè culture derives from biotechnical engineering, including those devices (or better, modified creatures) that serve in place of writing—"neurological image recorders." This is just as well, since the Yilanè language, worked out by Professor T. A. Shippey, is partly verbal and partly body English. The Yilanè social order, of course, is determined by the reproductive biology of reptiles: males are torpid during that part of the year when they carry the eggs, thus leaving the females the dominant sex by default. For some reason Harrison cannot explain, the facts of reptilian life have provoked angry letters from radical feminists. (Perhaps they prefer ideology to anatomy as the determinant of destiny.)

No part of Yilanè physiology is invented. These lizards are really alien because their biology is alien, not the least of their difference from us being their aversion to cold. This fact sets the story in motion. Yilanè centers of civilization are located mainly in Africa, with extensions into Europe and other northern parts of the Old World. But now a new Ice Age creeps onto the scene, bringing with it the pressures of climatic change and resource shortage, and the Yilanè are forced to explore and start to colonize the New World across the Atlantic Ocean. A new Ice Age *today?* Why not? Geologists are divided as to whether the Holocene is really a postglacial epoch or just another interglacial waiting upon the next movement of the ice. Perhaps the onset of a fifth after the Würm glaciation has been speeded up, given the long-range effects on the world's climate of that nonevent of sixty-five million years ago. But no matter; it is a necessary fiction.

So is the fact that North America still is occupied by a late Pleistocene or Wisconsin fauna (the same as the Würm fauna of Europe but not in the Europe of this parallel world), including giant deer, sabre-toothed tigers, and woolly mastodons. How else can the author give the proper romantic gloss to the Saurolithic Age about to reveal itself to the Stone Age hunters who also live here? And to the Yilanè as well? Then begins the war between the two species to eliminate each other from the face of the Earth, each thinking the enemy to be bestial and without intelligence.

But how did humans originate in the New World in this fiction? Man is an

Old World primate holding a common ancestry with the African apes (gorilla and chimpanzee) dating back to the Miocene epoch. Primate evolution in the New World broke off its affinities to that in the Old World about fifty-five million years ago, in the deeps of the Eocene epoch, just as ancestral monkeys were forming out of the prosimians. Thus in tropical South America, primate radiation was confined to prosimians and monkeys; no higher primates—no apes or hominids—appeared.

This difficulty is not insuperable, for it is possible to imagine a different outcome with only a slightly different throw of the Darwinian dice. In Africa, the first apelike primates begin to show up in the fossil record of the Oligocene epoch; they are quite small and can be distinguished from their monkey ancestors only by the five cusps on their molar teeth, four cusps being diagnostic of monkeys. Among the living primates a further distinction can be seen in the fact that monkeys, Old World and New, have tails and apes do not; but nothing of this is possible to know from a fossil record limited to teeth and jaw fragments. At all events, the first dubious hominids, together with enlarged apes, do not appear until the Miocene; I write dubious because the only evidence is that of five-cusped molars (hence man's closer affinity to apes than to monkeys) arranged in jaw bones, much fragmented and distorted, that seem to be curved in the human way (parabolic and not U-shaped as with living and fossil apes). By the time skulls and long bones are found in the Pliocene record, the apeman ancestors of genus *Homo* are unambiguously established; but how far back the hominid line goes, and at what point it branches off from the proto-apes—all that remains completely in the dark. The most likely story is that both the hominid and the ape line branched off together from the proto-monkeys at about the same time the latter branched off from the prosimians.

This allows for the fictive evolution of a hominid line out of the proto-monkeys of the Eocene epoch in South America. It really is not necessary to have apes on the scene—they are human collaterals, not ancestors. Thus Harrison is free to imagine proto-monkey ancestors for his New World humans (indeed, they have vestigial tails), just as in the Old World, the only difference being that they did not give rise as well to apes at the same branching-off point. All this is more than plausible in the alternative world westward of Eden.

When the story opens, the Yilanè have not yet reached the western hemisphere. The human realm is confined to North America and is limited to the Tanu and the Paramutan, both hunting cultures, but South and Central America are occupied by unintelligent saurians that are called "the Wild Ones." The Paramutin, as already mentioned, is Eskimo-like in its Mesolithic state of culture, but with no outside Neolithic source for its crucial technology. It would be easy to provide one, since the Neolithic arose independently out of the Mesolithic more than once in the Old World. So perhaps the Paramutin may, after all, be granted the necessaries on their own. The Tanu are big-game hunters with an Upper Paleolithic technology as is appropriate, but with the addition of the Mesolithic bow and arrow, a not unreasonable mix for an alternate-world development. Altogether the two cultures are quite workable ones, consistent with their lithic "age," unlike the inauthentic primitivity that Harrison has indulged previously. In this case, Harrison dutifully did the homework assigned him.[4]

The narrator of the story is Kerrick of the Tanu, who as a boy was captured by the Yilanè and raised by them, only to escape and then to lead his people against them. Some reviewers have noted that, for three volumes— *West of Eden* (1984), *Winter in Eden* (1986), and *Return to Eden* (1988)— there is more "world" than story to this narrative. But that complaint misses the point.

The real narrative subject of the trilogy *is* that world. Like the Middle-earth of J. R. R. Tolkien's *Lord of the Rings* trilogy, a cult book Harrison means to rival with his, the world "West of Eden" is one intended for the reader's total immersion. He is meant to plunge into this world, there to live and experience it. To that end the book contains maps and each chapter is headed with a fine scratch-board illustration by Bill Sanderson, who also did the illustrated "Zoology" for the appendices. These also include dictionaries, a history of the Yilanè, and accounts of their physiology, diet, reproductive biology, science, language, and culture.

And so, for once, does the Saurolithic Age come to life with valid credentials. By sticking to his belief that science fiction is at its best when keeping faith with science, Harrison has achieved a triumphant work of the imagination.

Harry Harrison So Far

In my account of the *West of Eden* trilogy, I have stressed more of its anthropology than is visible to the reader's eye, or is meant to be. Harrison's art is the art that conceals art, yet all of the matters touched upon went into shaping the project from the outset, as I know from being one of his consultants. Harrison digested all this information in his own way, with the result that he has created a parallel world of faultless internal consistency. How the artistic effect was achieved is possible to glimpse, it is hoped, from some of the work's hidden profundities here revealed. Indeed, my approach in this chap-

ter has been to probe behind the scenes, much as do students of J. R. R.
Tolkien in explicating the historical and literary background of his
Middle-earth.[5]

But the impression I wish to leave with the reader is the extreme care
Harrison takes in researching the science in what the pulp magazine industry
since 1926 has called science fiction; for although it is at bottom a genre of
romance, he is more convinced than most writers of science fiction that its
fantastic or speculative element is the more entertaining when it also appeals
to veracity. Combining the romantic with the realistic calls for unusual discipline, but Harrison's mastery of his craft has been rewarded, in *West of Eden*,
with a work that to date has most satisfied his own long held conception of
what science fiction could and should be.

West of Eden can also be seen as the natural outgrowth of his expanding career. As ever, he is didactic when it comes to the Enlightenment values of science, which serve him not only as the grounding of his research but also as the
instructive content of the story itself. (For example, the more visible Yilanè
science of genetics and its application to biotechnology[6] is meant to teach
something about these fields in particular, but also to cultivate habits of rational thought in general.) But this reversion to technophilic science fiction,
the genre's oldest tradition, does not stand alone; it is the foundation on
which he builds a sophisticated superstructure in the best tradition of social
science fiction, carried forward by a narrative vigor that owes to his unique
and intelligent handling of the adventure story—the basic American genre
established long before the advent of a special-interest readership for science
fiction as a publisher's category. This fluent mix has increasingly brought
him a wider audience that transcends the science fiction market. It is also the
basis for my analysis of Harry Harrison as a significant American writer.
Moreover, I hope this book will awaken further interest, as he proceeds to un-
fold yet new adventures, from a critical community that has ignored him far
too long.

Notes and References

Chapter One

1. This first part of the chapter is a reprint (with a few editorial changes) of Leon Stover, "Science Fiction and the Research Revolution," in *Teaching Science Fiction*, ed. Jack Williamson (Philadelphia: Owlswick Press, 1980), 33–37. It was originally delivered as the Distinguished Faculty Lecture to the Society of Sigma Xi, at the Illinois Institute of Technology on 18 April 1978.

2. Leon Stover, "Social Science Fiction," in Williamson, *Teaching Science Fiction*, 137–44.

3. Merlin Thomas, *Louis-Ferdinand Céline* (New York: New Directions, 1979), 67. Thomas writes about Marquis (the pseudonymn of Henri de Graffigny) because he was a friend of Céline.

4. On the sad history of Verne in English, see Walter Miller's preface to his authentic translation of *Twenty Thousand Leagues under the Sea* (New York: Washington Square Press, 1965), vii–xxii. See also the foreword to his newly rendered and annotated edition of *From the Earth to the Moon* (New York: Thomas Y. Crowell, 1978), ix–xix.

5. For further details, see Leon Stover, "Jules Verne," in *Twentieth-Century Science-Fiction Writers*, 2d ed., ed. Curtis C. Smith (Chicago: St. James Press, 1986), 855f. See also Jean Chesneaux, *The Political and Social Ideas of Jules Verne* (London: Thames and Hudson, 1972).

6. See Leon Stover, *The Prophetic Soul: A Reading of H. G. Wells's "Things to Come"* (Jefferson, N.C.: McFarland, 1987), esp. 86.

7. H. G. Wells, *Experiment in Autobiography* (New York: Macmillan, 1934), 558.

8. Patrick Parrinder and Robert Philmus, eds., *H. G. Wells's Literary Criticism* (Brighton, England: Harvester Press, 1980), 224f.

9. "Machine as Hero," in Robert Holdstock, consultant ed., *Encyclopedia of Science Fiction* (London: Octopus Books, 1978), 86–103.

Chapter Two

1. "Humanism," in *A Dictionary of Christian Theology*, ed. Alan Richardson (Philadelphia: Westminister Press, 1969), 161f.; Max Otto, "Scientific Humanism," chapter 9 in *Science and the Moral Life* (New York: Mentor Books, 1949), originally published in *Antioch Review* (Winter 1943). Harry Harrison himself ap-

pears in the British *Humanist* (October 1961) with the article "Science Fiction Comes of Age."

2. See "Conventions," "Horning, Charles D.," and "Science Fiction League," in *The Science Fiction Encyclopedia*, ed. Peter Nicholls (Garden City, N.Y.: Doubleday, 1979), 138, 292f., and 525.

3. See "Moskowitz, Sam(uel)," in Nicholls, *The Science Fiction Encyclopedia*, 410.

4. Russel B. Nye, *The Unembarrassed Muse: The Popular Arts in America* (New York: Dial Press, 1970), 240.

5. "The Beginning of the Affair," in *Hell's Cartographers*, ed. Brian Aldiss and Harry Harrison (London: Orbit Books, 1976), 80.

6. Frederik Pohl, *The Way the Future Was: A Memoir* (London: Victor Gollancz, 1979), plate, op. 160, caption under top left photo.

7. See "Comic Strips and Comic Books," in Nicholls, *The Science Fiction Encyclopedia*, 130–31.

8. For brief entries on these titles, see Nicholls, *The Science Fiction Encyclopedia*, under their alphabetical listings. Cameron Hall, as noted, is the house editorial name used by Harrison.

9. For other choice examples, see Harrison, *Hell's Cartographers*, 82.

10. From *Locus 90* (12 July 1971):9.

11. For my own estimate of Campbell, see Leon Stover, "The Meaning of John Campbell," in *Métaphores* 7 (France: University of Nice, 1983), 117–31. See also Leon Stover, "John W. Campbell," in Curtis C. Smith, ed., *Twentieth-Century Science-Fiction Writers*, 2d ed. (Chicago: St. James Press, 1986), 115–16.

12. For a catalogue of all films in the series, consult James Gunn, "The Tinsel Screen: Science Fiction and the Movies," in Williamson, *Teaching Science Fiction*, 215–17.

13. Kingsley Amis and Robert Conquest, eds., *Spectrum 5* (New York: Berkley Medallion Books, 1966), 12.

14. Header to "The Mothballed Spaceship," in *Astounding: John W. Campbell Memorial Anthology*, ed. Harry Harrison (New York: Random House, 1973), 205.

15. *Hell's Cartographers*, 94.

16. "Jim Burns," in Robert Jackson, ed., *Frontier Crossings*, a souvenir of the 45th World Science Fiction Convention: Conspiracy '87, Brighton, England, 27 August to 1 September 1987 (London: Science Fiction Conventions, 1987), 84f. A written "Self Portrait" by Jim Burns himself appears on 86f.

17. Frederik Pohl, "The Science Fiction Professional," in *The Craft of Science Fiction*, ed. Reginold Bretnor (New York: Barnes and Noble Books, 1976), 293.

18. Actually (as Harrison explains), the proper name is Writers Guild of America West [Hollywood], to distinguish it from Writers Guild of America, which is eastern and theatrical.

19. See Elizabeth Anne Hull, "SF Conference in Moscow," in *SFRA Newsletter* 153 (November–December 1987):4–6. The one disappointing note, to my

mind, was the inevitable peace petition, a declaration titled "Science Fiction and the Future of Mankind" (5f.). It was composed by science fiction brains from seventeen countries, not counting the Soviet Union, and its platitudes are indistinguishable from those of the World Council of Churches. For a sampling, see John Rees, ed., *The War Called Peace: The Soviet Peace Offensive* (Alexandria, Va.: Western Goals; 1982). I often wonder why those writers who stress the science in science fiction have never once turned from sentimental humanitarianism to play with the ideas expressed by Raymond B. Cattel in *A New Morality from Science: Beyondism* (New York: Pergamon Press, 1972). Note added in press: Harrison tells me that the declaration was composed by himself and Fred Pohl.

20. *World SF Newsletter* 2 (August 1988):3.

21. The conference was hosted by Corpus Christi State University, Texas, 30 June–3 July 1988.

22. Published in Peter Nicholls, ed., *Science Fiction At Large* (London: Gollancz, 1976; New York: Harper & Row, 1977).

23. "The State of Science Fiction," in *Bulletin of the Science Fiction Writers of America* 95 (Spring 1987):38.

24. Arthur O. Lewis, in *Fantasy Review* 95 (October 1986):25.

Chapter Three

1. It was Boyle who made a science of chemistry out of alchemy, at the same time he made science a religious way of life. As an activist in the English Revolution on the side of the Puritans against priestcraft and absolutism, he found chemistry his way of serving God. "Experimental philosophy, the procedure of science, teaches religious truth by furnishing a model of how to live" (from J. R. Jacob, *Robert Boyle and the English Revolution* [New York: Burt Franklin, 1977], 179). On the common assumptions of the Enlightenment as a movement for social and political change, see C. B. A. Behrens, *Society, Government, and the Enlightenment* (New York: Harper & Row, 1985), part 3, 152–62.

2. *The Best of Harry Harrison* (London: Futura Publications, 1976), 40.

3. Voltaire, *Philosophical Dictionary*, trans. Theodore Besterman (Harmondsworth: Penguin Books, 1972), 329.

4. D. H. Lawrence, as quoted by James Gunn, "Science Fiction and the Mainstream," in *Science Fiction, Today and Tomorrow*, ed. Reginold Bretnor (Baltimore: Penguin Books, 1974), 202.

5. F. R. Leavis, as quoted by James Gunn, in *Science Fiction, Today and Tomorrow*, 203. See also blurb on back of Damon Knight, ed., *Cities of Wonder* (New York: Macfadden Books, 1967).

6. Ezra Pound, as quoted by R. H. Stacy, in *Defamiliarization in Language and Literature* (Syracuse, N.Y.: Syracuse University Press, 1977), 2.

7. From publisher's advertisement on the back of the American paperback edition of *Planet of the Damned* (New York: Bantam Books, 1962). It was probably

written by Harrison himself, as is also likely in the case of the blurb cited later from *Planet of No Return* (New York: Tor Books, 1982).

8. Leon Stover, "The Meaning of John W. Campbell," in *Métaphores* 7, 124f., 129.

9. Bertrand Russell under the given chapter title from his book of 1931, *Scientific Outlook*, quoted by F. A. Hayek, in *The Counter-Revolution of Science: Studies on the Abuse of Reason*, 2d ed. (Indianapolis: Liberty Press, 1979), 179. The statist ethic of modern liberalism has its more widely accepted credentials from Karl Mannheim, as expressed in *Man and Society in an Age of Reconstruction* (London: Kegan Paul, 1940).

10. In Han Stefan Santesson, ed., *Rulers of Men* (New York: Pyramid Books, 1965), 135–59.

11. Bertrand Russell, quoted in Hayek, *The Counter-Revolution of Science*, 179.

12. Robert Nisbet, *Prejudices, a Philosophical Dictionary* (Cambridge: Harvard University Press, 1982), 217. The image of the stars as a symbol of freedom from war is traceable to Henry Vaughan, one of the seventeenth-century metaphysical poets, whose "Peace" opens with these lines:

> My soul, there is a country
>   Far beyond the stars,
> Where stands a wingèd sentry
>   All skilful in the wars:
> There, above noise and danger,
>   Sweet Peace sits crown'd with smiles.

This image comes complete with coercive angel, sword of peace in hand, ready to enforce that freedom.

13. Reprinted in H. Bruce Franklin, ed., *Future Perfect: American Science Fiction of the Nineteenth Century* (New York: Oxford University Press, 1966), 368–73.

14. Published in the original French as *La Guerre du Feu*, and translated into English by Harold Talbott for Pantheon Books (Random House) in 1967.

15. See Nicholls, *The Science Fiction Encyclopedia*, 44, column 1, under "Asimov, Isaac."

16. While faster-than-light travel remains remotely conceivable as a means of getting from planet to distant planet, matter transmission—despite "Star Trek: The New Generation"—is totally out of the question. See Peter Nicholls, "Matter Transmission," in *The Science in Science Fiction* (New York: Alfred A. Knopf, 1983), 135.

17. H. G. Wells, *A Modern Utopia* (London: Chapman and Hall, 1905), 144. For a reprint of this edition see Bison Books (Lincoln, Nebraska: University of Nebraska Press, 1967).

18. *One Step from Earth* (New York: Macmillan, 1970), 171. See also in *The Best of Harry Harrison* (London: Futura Publications, 1976), 154.

Chapter Four

1. Cited by John Baxter, in *Science Fiction in the Cinema* (New York: Paperback Library, 1970), 44.
2. Mark R. Hillegas, *The Future as Nightmare: H. G. Wells and the Anti-Utopians* (New York: Oxford University Press, 1967). In my judgment, however, Hillegas is wrong about Wells (although not about the rest). See Stover, *The Prophetic Soul*, esp. 106, n. 16, on *When the Sleeper Wakes* (1899), the key novel in the estimate of Wellsian science fiction as dystopian.
3. "Conceptual Breakthrough," in Nicholls, *The Science Fiction Encyclopedia*, 134–37. But this is just jargon for a plot element favored by Aristotle, the discovery or recognition (*anagnorisis*) whereby a character suddenly gains the vital knowledge he lacks, the real identity of other characters, or, as it may be, some profound insight. See Marlies K. Danziger and Wendell Stacy Johnson, *The Critical Reader: Analyzing and Judging Literature* (New York: Frederick Ungar, 1978), 91.
4. See Lawrence S. Lerner and Edward A. Gosselin, "Galileo and the Spector of Bruno," *Scientific American* 255 (November 1986):126–33.
5. Gilbert Highet, review of *Captive Universe, Book-of-the-Month Club News*, April 1969, 8.

Chapter Five

1. See introduction to Magnus Magnusson and Herman Pálsson, trans., *The Vinland Sagas: The Norse Discovery of America* (Baltimore: Penguin Books, 1965). The second saga in this book, that of Eirik the Red, is the one to read for a studied appreciation of the comic use Harrison has made of Thorfinn Karlsefni's life, including his marriage to Gudrid (who in the novel is the Hollywood sex goddess playing the part and who, at the film's completion, returns home to Greenland with "Ottar" to bear the children of his recorded lineage).
2. Something Harrison did not tell me about was his early professional interest in black culture, which I came upon thanks to the bibliographic researches of Paul Tomlinson. See Harry Harrison, *The Complete Life of Lena Horne: A Pocket Celebrity Scrapbook*, no. 8 (New York: Pocket Magazines, 1955).
3. Fletcher Pratt, *Ordeal by Fire* (New York: Sloane Associates, 1948); reprint, *A Short History of the Civil War* (New York: Pocket Books, 1952). Pratt (d. 1956) was a historian of military Americana, one of the pioneer names in magazine science fiction, whose former works are much loved by Harrison's generation of writers as technical and historical source books, and a close friend of Harrison. In rereading *Ordeal by Fire* with the Civil War novel in mind, Harrison discovered "The key to the story!" when he noted John Brown's raid missing from it, alone among all the many books on the subject.

4. In Nicholls, *Science Fiction at Large*. See also "Alternate Worlds" and "Parallel Worlds" in Nicholls, *The Science Fiction Encyclopedia*.

5. This is the title of the ASF serialization (April, May, June 1972). The title of the original American book publication is *Tunnel through the Deeps* (New York: Putnam, 1972). But the magazine version of the title was restored in the American paperback edition (New York: Tor Books, 1972), as it was to the British hardcover edition (London: Faber & Faber, 1972).

6. "The Wicked Flee," for example, is a pilot story for *Transatlantic Tunnel*; "Down to Earth" is a type A story; "Secret of Stonehenge" is complicated type B; "Famous First Words" belongs with time travel by other means (radio). Best of all is "If," the definitive parody of all those cute stories about the alien from another dimension who opens the way for his kind in the here and now by pleading his case as a human refugee from a horrible future.

7. Geoffrey West, *H. G. Wells* (London: Gerald Howe, 1930), 294f.; Terry Ramsaye, "Robert Paul and *The Time Machine*," in *A Million and One Nights* (New York: Simon & Schuster, 1926). This latter chapter title is reprinted as appendix 9 in Harry M. Geduld, ed., *The Definitive Time Machine: A Critical Edition of H. G. Wells's Scientific Romance* (Bloomington: Indiana University Press, 1987), 196–203.

Chapter Six

1. On the distinctions made here, see the entries "burlesque" and "humor", in H. W. Fowler, *A Dictionary of Modern English Usage* (Kingsport, Tennessee: Oxford University Press, 1944), 59 and 249f.

2. Robert Heinlein won the first Grand Master Award from Science Fiction Writers of America in 1975; *Starship Troopers* won the Hugo Award in 1960.

3. "Machine as Hero," 95.

4. George W. Barlow, "Ringard de Choc ou L'Humour Hybride de Harry Harrison," *Proxima* 66 (1986):44–56.

5. James Burnam, *Suicide of the West: An Essay on the Meaning and Destiny of Liberalism* (1964; Chicago: Regnery Books, 1985), 240.

6. Also relevant here is a recently translated surviving fragment of Céline's *Casse-pipe*, which tells of his experience as a raw recruit on the first evening of his enrollment, on 28 September 1912, in the 12th Armored Cavalry. See *Cannon Fodder*, trans. K. De Coninck and B. Childish (Rochester, England: Hangman Books, 1988).

7. Chairman's introductory address in souvenir program, *1st World Science Fiction Writers Conference* (Dublin, Ireland: Pronto Print, 1976), 3.

8. Alan Greene, "*Star Smashers of the Galaxy Rangers*—Review," in *Parallel Worlds* 2 (Summer 1986):9–14. For details on this fanzine, see the Selected Bibliography.

9. Paul Tomlinson, "Space Opera!," in *Parallel Worlds* 2, 7f. [Editor's note: Tomlinson may identify the origin of the term "space opera," but his account of its

predecessors needs modification. The term "horse opera" originated first in silent film days for early Western films like Bill Hart's that were accompanied by grandiose piano improvisations, often using operatic material like the "Overture" to Rossini's *William Tell*. The term "soap opera" was applied in the 1930s to radio soapers because of their accompaniment by similar melodramatic music.]

10. See "Tucker, (Arthur) Wilson" in Nicholls, *The Science Fiction Encyclopedia*, 614f.

Chapter Seven

1. I remember discussing "horror sociology" with Professor Vernier at the 1972 meeting of the Association Française D'Études Américaines held in Dourdon, France, but I am unable to recall where he used the phrase in print. But for the idea of it, see Jean-Pierre Vernier, "H. G. Wells, Writer or Thinker? From Science Fiction to Social Prophecy," *Wellsian* 3 (Spring 1980):24–34. His view is that Wells's works of nonfiction, in the realm of crisis-mongering and social prophecy, "remain so readable today [because] they are so profoundly fictions" (34).

2. The birth rate is expressed as a quantity per 1000 of population, with 2.1 indicating equilibrium. On the cultural aspects of demographic decline, see Tom Wolfe (who holds a Ph.D. in sociology), Class Day Address at Harvard University, "The New Cookie, the Second Shoe, and the Final Freedom," excerpted in *Harvard Magazine* 90, no. 6 (July/August 1988):63.

3. See especially Harry Harrison, "A Cannibalized Novel Becomes *Soylent Green*," in *Omni's Screen Flights/Screen Fantasies: The Future According to Science Fiction Cinema*, ed. Danny Peary (Garden City, N.Y.: Doubleday, 1984), 143–46. See also the interview with Harrison about *Soylent Green* in John Brosnan, *Future Tense: The Cinema of Science Fiction* (New York: St. Martin's Press, 1978), 285–87. For Brosnan's own discussion of the film, see 202–9. Harrison's forward to the Brosnan book gives his views on the general inadequacies of science fiction films as a genre. During our Cornwall interviews, Harrison summed up Hollywood science fiction in the phrase, "Flashing lights, strange sounds, and incomprehensible language." The proximate cause of this witticism was *Close Encounters of the Third Kind* (1977), in which the reference object of his third term is the film's shoptalk in French, emblematic of the industry's policy in presenting "science as incomprehensible."

4. See Northrop Frye, *Anatomy of Criticism* (Princeton: Princeton University Press, 1957), 45.

5. Jonathan Kaufman, as quoted in Joan Beck's column, "Is the Black-Jewish Alliance Broken Beyond Repair?," in *Chicago Tribune*, (10 October 1988), 21.

6. Glenn C. Loury, "This Is Serfdom, Not Freedom," op-ed. page of *Chicago Tribune*, (29 April 1987). Excerpted from "Matters of Color—Blacks and the Constitutional Order," *Public Interest* (Winter 1987).

7. In Harry Harrison, ed., *The Year 2000* (Garden City, N.Y.: Doubleday, 1970), 263–82. The bitter alarmism of "American Dead" is very much a product of

the 1960s and is as much a striking period piece as is John Brunner's related novel of 1969, *The Jagged Orbit*. Brunner, however, treats the personal arms race in a mood of black comedy; otherwise the near-future setting is the same, a culturally fragmented United States whose freedom-loving citizens are armed with heavy weapons and have made fortresses of their homes.

8. In Bryon Preiss, ed., *The Planets* (New York: Bantam, 1985), 49–62. "After the Storm" is the story about Earth in a collection that features a nonfiction article and a short story for each planet of the Solar System.

Chapter Eight

1. For exhaustive research on all things pertaining to *Vendetta for the Saint*, see *Parallel Worlds*, no. 4. This 1987 issue of the fanzine of the Harry Harrison Appreciation Society contains a special eight-page insert, *The Parallel Worlds Mystery Magazine*, no. 1. It consists of three pieces by Paul Tomlinson: an article entitled "The Story of the Saint," a review of the novel, and an interview with Harrison about how he came to write it. The editorial, on the inside facing page of this unpaginated booklet, mentions three short stories written by Harrison under the name of Leslie Charteris, all published in *The Saint Mystery Magazine*. They are "Hitch-Hiker" (December 1959), "Terror in Tivoli" (August 1962), and "Case of the Cosmic Killer" (January 1966).

2. Patrick Anderson, "King of the 'Techno-Thriller,' " *New York Times Magazine*, (1 May 1988), 85.

3. Full-page ad placed by Faber & Faber in *1st World SF Writers Conference*, 15.

Chapter Nine

1. See "Where 'The Stainless Steel Rat' Began," in *Parallel Worlds* 3 (1986):18f.

2. Alan Greene, "The Thief as Hero," *Parallel Worlds* 3 (1986):4–8.

3. Ray Mosley, "Artificial Language Turns 100," *Chicago Tribune*, (12 July 1987, 6; David Diringer, *The Alphabet*, 2d ed. (New York: Philosophical Library, 1948), 559.

4. "Ni venos, Doktoro Zamenhof, ni venos!," in *Literatura Foiro* 111 (February 1988):10–15. This title can be translated into English as, "We Are Coming, Dr. Zamenhof, We Are Coming!"

5. It is futile to argue that much more is needed than a shared language to bring about universal amity and to end war—witness the American Civil War, with English spoken on both sides. These facts are as plain to Esperanto enthusiasts as to anybody else. What, then, is its mystique? Probably antinationalism. Nations (once they settle their civil wars) are bounded political communities, more or less part of some international community that is not a real community, and that is why diplomacy is the operational word in the international sphere and not politics, as this other word applies within the nation states. Thus the noncommunity at large is an attrac-

tive void to be filled, in dreamy anticipation, with the same regularized politics and linguistic unities that bind the genuine but disesteemed national communities. Or rather, international unison, not yet realized, promises to be even more authentic than nationalism because undivided. Meanwhile, good diplomacy is not good enough.

    6. See Jack Katz, *Seductions of Crime* (New York: Basic Books, 1988).

Chapter Ten

    1. On *The Santaroga Barrier,* see Leon Stover, "Social Science Fiction," 140–42.

    2. John W. Campbell, introduction to Robert A. Heinlein, *The Man Who Sold the Moon* (New York: Mentor Books, 1951), viii.

    3. See Jeffrey Gantz, *Early Irish Myths and Sagas* (Harmondsworth, England: Penguin Books, 1981), 3f. Here the term used is "formative Celts" in place of my "proto-Celts."

    4. For Brian Aldiss's negative review of the film, see the *Guardian*, 21 July 1971, 8.

    5. See Erik v. Kuehnelt-Leddihn, "Paradise Lost," in *National Review* 40, no. 24 (9 December 1988):24. On the Scandinavian trade-off between statism and cultural license, see Roland Huntford, *The New Totalitarians* (New York: Stein & Day, 1972).

    6. Quoted in Robert Philmus and David Y. Hughs, eds., *Early Writings in Science and Science Fiction by H. G. Wells* (Berkeley and Los Angeles: University of California Press, 1975), 180, n. 3.

    7. This often overlooked point is examined by Benjamin Hart, *Faith and Freedom: The Christian Roots of American Liberty* (Dallas, Texas: Lewis & Stanley, 1988).

    8. William Irwin Thompson, " 'We Become What We Hate, ' " op-ed page of the *New York Times*, 25 July 1971.) In terms of science fiction history, *Deathworld* builds on Eric Frank Russell's ASF story of 1941, "Symbiotica," a comic treatment of planetary ecology; it is a puzzle story in which finding the key organism in the ecological pyramid, or chain of life, is the basis for knockabout adventure. Harrison's novel, so acknowledged, is a sombre variant.

    9. Jerry Pournelle, "The Construction of Believable Societies," in Bretnor; *The Craft of Science Fiction*, 106f.

    10. Bernard Gert, *The Moral Rules* (New York: Harper & Row, 1970). His ten moral rules, as generalized to cover the particularities of each case, are listed as follows opposite the title page (ranked by importance in two sets).

The First Five	*The Second Five*
1. Don't kill.	6. Don't deceive.
2. Don't cause pain.	7. Keep your promise.
3. Don't disable.	8. Don't cheat.

4. Don't deprive of freedom or   9. Obey the law.
   opportunity
5. Don't deprive of pleasure.   10. Do your duty.

11. C. S. Lewis, *The Abolition of Man* (New York: Macmillan, 1947), 61. On natural law and positive law, see Thomas Fleming, *The Politics of Human Nature* (New Brunswick, N.J.: Transaction Books, 1988), chapter 3. It should be added here that some of the more bizarre examples of human conduct, used to attack the concept of natural law, are drawn from such benighted cultures, doomed by surrounding powerful states, that they may well be called "concentration-camp cultures" (as indeed they were called by my professors in graduate school).

Chapter Eleven

1. On the films in question, see Baxter, *Science Fiction in the Cinema*; Brosnan, *Future Tense*; Peary, *Omini's Screen Flights*; David Shipman, *A Pictorial History of Science Fiction Films* (Twickenham, England: Hamlyn, 1985); and Philip Strick, *Science Fiction Movies* (London: Octopus Books, 1976). On Conan Doyle, Captain Adam Seaborn (the real name of John Cleves Symmnes), E. R. Burroughs, and the "lost world" theme, see alphabetical entries in Nicholls, *The Science Fiction Encyclopedia*. Here also are entries for R. H. Rosny and Stanley Waterloo.

2. See Carroll L. Riley, J. Charles Kelly, Campbell W. Pennington, and Robert L. Rands, eds., *Man across the Sea: Problems of Pre-Columbian Contact* (Austin: University of Texas Press, 1971). It is evident in the alternate world of the *West of Eden* trilogy that all tropical and semitropical zones have been more or less dominated by reptiles from the Cretaceous into the Tertiary and Quaternary periods, including the areas of our world's Latin America where the Aztec, Maya, and Inca civilizations arose. In *West of Eden* their rise is impossible, both as a localized event and as one with connections, however tenuous, with prior developments in the Old World, where a saurian rather than a human civilization came into being. Human evolution, with the possibilities of human culture, could not have occurred as it did in our world's African cradle, as it is preempted in *West of Eden* by reptilian evolution, at first biological and then cultural to the complete domination of Africa and most of Eurasia. But it does occur in the New World (before it is reached by saurian civilization), where man is allowed his chances from a starting point among the lower primates in a tropical niche of their own ecological preserve, left open by less advanced reptiles. He then moves himself northward to an area of reptile-free cold, and then establishes a hunting culture.

For the sake of precision, I should add that the New World civilizations, as we know them from the archeological record, were not uniformly literate. While the Aztecs had a pictographic and the Mayas an ideographic system of writing, the Incas lacked *any* system of writing, although a functional equivalent is to be seen in their knotted-string records, or *quipus*. Thus wheeled transport is the only technology missing from an old world-based definition of civilization.

3. For example, see Malcom W. Browne, "Debate over Dinosaur Extinction Takes an Unusually Rancorous Turn," in the *New York Times*, 19 January 1988, 19, 23. This was followed on 6 February 1988 by heated exchanges in the Letters column. The *Times* earlier (19 December 1987) ran an editorial on the subject, "Did Dinosaurs Die a Dull Death?"

4. Principally Carleton S. Coon, *The Hunting Peoples* (Boston: Little, Brown, 1971). Those reviewers who claimed that Harrison's Tanu and Paramutan are not realistic might profit by reading Coon. The same reviewers claim Yilanè culture (or civilization) to be an absurdity; but as they are also the ones who think the story laid in the Alley Oop past, they are not to be taken seriously. For Harrison's one published reply to such nonsense, see "The World West of Eden," *Fantasy Review* 74 (December 1984):13.

5. See, for example, Paul H. Kocher, *Master of Middle-Earth* (Boston: Houghton Mifflin, 1972).

6. It is important to note that biotechnology, in the field of genetic engineering, provides the Yilanè with the functional equivalents of those three inventions that define the emergence of civilization in terms of material culture: wheel making, writing, and metal working.

Selected Bibliography

PRIMARY WORKS

I have not attempted in the following list to catalog Harrison's more than fifty anthologies; the most important are mentioned in chapter 2.

Short Story Collections

Story titles in parentheses are alternative ones used in magazine publication. Limited space forbids listing magazine sources, or Harrison's many uncollected stories. For the latter, see Curtis C. Smith under Secondary Works. Collection titles are listed alphabetically. First editions are the rule, the place of publication is New York City unless otherwise noted.

The Best of Harry Harrison. Pocket Books, 1976.
  "The Streets of Ashkelon" ("An Alien Agony"); "Captain Honario Harpplayer, RN"; "Rescue Operation"; "At Last, the True Story of Frankenstein"; "I Always Do What Teddy Says"; "Portrait of the Artist"; "Mute Milton"; "A Criminal Act"; "Waiting Place"; "If" ("Praiseworthy Saur"); "I Have My Vigil"; "From Fanaticism, or for Reward"; "By the Falls"; "The Ever-branching Tree"; "The Wicked Flee"; "Roommates"; "The Mothballed Spaceship"; "An Honest Day's Work"; "We Ate the Whole Thing"; "Space Rats of the CCC."
One Step from Earth. Macmillan, 1970.
  "Introduction—The Matter Transmitter"; "One Step from Earth"; "No War, or Battle's Sound" ("Or Battle's Sound"); "Wife to the Lord"; "Waiting Place"; "The Life Preservers"; "From Fanaticism, or for Reward"; "Heavy Duty"; "A Tale of the Ending."
Prime Number. Berkley Books, 1970.
  "Mute Milton"; "The Greatest Car in the World"; "The Final Battle"; "The Powers of Observation"; "The Ghoul Squad"; "Toy Shop"; "You Men of Violence"; "The Finest Hunter in the World"; "Down to Earth"; "Commando Raid"; "Not Me, Not Amos Cabot!"; "The Secret of Stonehenge"; "Incident on the IND"; "If"; "Contact Man"; "The Pad"; "A Civil Servant" ("The Fairly Civil Servant"); "A Criminal Act"; "Famous First Words."
Two Tales and Eight Tomorrows. Gollancz (London), 1965.
  "The Streets of Ashkelon"; "Portrait of the Artist"; "Rescue Operation"; "Captain Bedlam"; "Final Encounter"; "Unto My Manifold Dooms" ("The Many

Dooms"); "The Pliable Animal"; "Captain Horatio Harpplayer, RN"; "According to His Abilities"; "I Always Do What Teddy Says."
War with the Robots. Pyramid Books, 1962.
"A Word From the (Human) Author"; "Simulated Trainer" ("Trainee for Mars"); "The Velvet Glove"; "Arm of the Law"; "The Robot Who Wanted to Know"; "I See You" ("Robot of Justice"); "The Repairman"; "Survival Planet"; "War with the Robots."

Novels

I cite the first American editions (New York), but make one exception to accommodate a British title whose wording is used in chapter 5. Magazine sources for the serialized versions and their frequently variant titles have been indicated where appropriate throughout this book, and are not repeated here.

Bill, the Galactic Hero. Doubleday, 1965.
Captive Universe. Putnam, 1969.
Deathworld. Bantam Books, 1960.
Deathworld 2. Bantam Books, 1964.
Deathworld 3. Dell Books, 1968.
The Deathworld Trilogy. Berkley Books, 1976.
The Daleth Effect. Putnam, 1970.
Homeworld (*To the Stars*, part 1). Bantam Books, 1980.
Invasion Earth. Ace Books, 1982.
Plague from Space. Doubleday, 1965. Rewritten and expanded as *The Jupiter Plague.* Tor Books, 1982.
The Lifeship. With Gordon R. Dickson. Harper & Row, 1976.
Make Room! Make Room!. Doubleday, 1966.
Montezuma's Revenge. Doubleday, 1972.
Planet of the Damned. Bantam Books, 1962.
Planet of No Return. Tor Books, 1982.
The QE2 Is Missing. MacDonald-Futura, 1980.
Queen Victoria's Revenge. Doubleday, 1974.
Rebel in Time. Tor Books, 1983.
Return to Eden (*West of Eden*, part 3). Bantam, 1988.
Skyfall. Atheneum, 1977. First published in London by Faber in 1976.
A Stainless Steel Rat is Born. Bantam Books, 1985.
The Stainless Steel Rat. Pyramid Books, 1961.
The Stainless Steel Rat for President. Doubleday, 1982.
The Stainless Steel Rat Gets Drafted. Bantam, 1987.
The Stainless Steel Rat's Revenge. Walker, 1970.
The Stainless Steel Rat Saves the World. Putnam, 1972.
The Stainless Steel Rat Wants You. Doubleday, 1979.
Star Smashers of the Galaxy Rangers. Putnam, 1973.

Starworld (*To the Stars*, part 3). Bantam Books, 1981.
Stonehenge. With Leon Stover. Scribners, 1972.
Stonehenge: Where Atlantis Died. With Leon Stover. Tor Books, 1983.
The Technicolor Time Machine. Doubleday, 1967.
To the Stars. Doubleday, 1981.
A Transatlantic Tunnel, Hurrah!. Faber (London), 1972. This is the preferred title.
    Published in New York the same year by Putnam as *Tunnel through the Deeps*.
Vendetta for the Saint. Ghosted for Leslie Charteris. Doubleday, 1964.
West of Eden. Bantam, 1984.
Wheelworld (*To the Stars*, part 2). Bantam Books, 1981.
Winter in Eden (*West of Eden*, part 2). Bantam, 1986.

Juveniles

The California Iceberg. Walker, 1975.
The Men from P.I.G. and R.O.B.O.T.. Atheneum, 1978. Expanded version of *The
    Man from P.I.G.*, published by Avon Books in 1968.
Spaceship Medic. Doubleday, 1970.

Nonfiction and Miscellaneous

Great Balls of Fire: A History of Sex in SF. Grosset and Dunlap, 1977.
Mechanismo. Reed Books (Los Angeles), 1978.
Planet Story. Illustrated novel, with Jim Burns. A & W Visual (Englewood Cliffs,
    N.J.), 1979.
Spacecraft of Fact and Fiction. With Malcolm Edwards. Exeter, 1979.
You Can Be the Stainless Steel Rat. Interactive gamebook. Ace Books, 1988.

SECONDARY WORKS

No academic literature exists, although a professional interview, titled "Harry
Harrison," was conducted by Charles Platt for *Isaac Asimov's Science Fiction Maga-
zine* (August 1982), 28–40; reprinted in Platt, *Dream Makers*, vol. 2 (New York:
Berkey Books, 1983), 28–40.

A fanzine devoted to the author has been published in England by the Harry
Harrison Appreciation Society (Paul Tomlinson, 77 Belmont Road, Kirkby-in-
Ashfield, Nottingham U.K. NG17 9DY). Its first two issues (April and September
1985) were titled *Make Room!*. Subsequent issues (from 1986 to 1988) have been
numbered 1 through 6&7 under the title, *Parallel Worlds*. This fan magazine contains interviews with Harrison, reviews of his books, articles about various aspects of
his work, short topical notices, and news items, almost all the work of Paul

Tomlinson. In the intervals, Tomlinson sends out one-page newssheets, numbered 1–10 so far.

Another fan publication is Francesco Biamonti, *Harry Harrison: Bibliographia (1951–1965)*, privately printed in Trieste, Italy. It contains annotations by Harrison for each title.

For entries in general reference books, the following sources are the most important.

Aldiss, Brian W. *Trillion Year Spree: The True History of Science Fiction.* New York: Atheneum, 1986. A revision of *Billion Year Spree* (1973). Consult index.

Ash, Brian. *Who's Who in Science Fiction.* New York: Taplinger, 1976. A biobibliographic directory of about four hundred Science Fiction writers. Largely superceded by the superior Nicholls encyclopedia (see below).

Barron, Neil, ed. *Anatomy of Wonder: A Critical Guide to Science Fiction.* 3d ed. New York: Bowker, 1987. Contains critical reviews of twenty-three Harrison titles.

Nicholls, Peter, ed. *The Science Fiction Encyclopedia.* Garden City, N.Y.: Doubleday, 1979.

Smith, Curtis C., ed. *Twentieth-Century Science-Fiction Writers.* 2d ed. Chicago: St. James Press, 1986. The Harrison entry, prepared by this author, contains a complete list of the uncollected stories.

Index